DESIGNING AND PLANNING
BATHROOMS

CREATIVE HOMEOWNER PRESS®

CONTENTS

Based on *Creating a Home*
First Edition © Eaglemoss Publications Limited, 1986, 1987, 1988

Printed at Webcrafters, Inc.
Madison, Wisconsin, U.S.A.

Current printing (last digit)
10 9 8 7 6 5 4 3 2 1

Creative Director: Warren Ramezzana
Editor: Kimberly Kerrigone
Copy Editor: Carolyn Anderson-Feighner
Cover Photograph: Melabee M. Miller
Cover Interior Designer: Kathleen Dickelman, KAT Interior Designs
Design Consultant: Alan Asarnow, CKD, CR, Ulrich Inc.

Library of Congress Catalog Number: 91-071687
ISBN 0-932944-99-X (paper)

CREATIVE HOMEOWNER PRESS® BOOK SERIES
A DIVISION OF FEDERAL MARKETING CORP.
24 PARK WAY
UPPER SADDLE RIVER, NJ 07458-2311

INTRODUCTION

Whether you are planning a bathroom from scratch or just want to update what you have, this is the book to help you get the best results.

Designing and Planning Bathrooms starts off with a chapter on getting the basic planning right, followed by page after page of ideas for bathrooms to suit every taste and budget. There's the built-in bathroom, designed to provide plenty of storage space; new looks for old bathrooms; bathrooms featuring unusual decor or unconventional fixtures such as round or period style tubs; and super-modern ultra-streamlined bathrooms. Further chapters deal with more specialized rooms: fitness bathrooms equipped with whirlpools and saunas; shower stall rooms; master bathrooms; and powder rooms.

The bathroom is just the place to indulge a yen for way-out decor that would quickly tire in other rooms. This book is rich in examples of such fun bathrooms, designed to evoke, for example, a conservatory, a ship's cabin, a marble hall, even an Arabian night.

However, the practical side is given equal importance. Whatever the decor, fantastic, romantic or strictly functional, the materials used must be long lasting and stand up to water, steam and condensation. Further chapters show the best materials to use for walls and floors; how to plan creative but practical tiling schemes; and how to install a tub surround. Four buyers' guides illustrate the wide range of tub and shower stall fixtures on the market.

Designing and Planning Bathrooms is an essential ideas book and practical guide for anyone planning to redecorate or remodel a bathroom.

ORGANIZING YOUR BATHROOM

Think carefully about plumbing, heating and ventilation when planning your bathroom.

The bathroom should be one of the most inviting rooms in your home. Try to make it a combination of warmth and luxury with the practical plus points of easy-to-clean fixtures, accessories and splashproof wall and floorcoverings.

Relaxing in a hot bath, or enjoying an invigorating shower are both wonderful ways to unwind after a difficult day, but a chilly, badly decorated bathroom is no place to linger. Often a coat of paint, some thick, foam-backed carpet, fluffy towels and the addition of a heated towel rail can make the difference between discomfort and welcoming warmth. If the room is old and in poor condition or the plumbing is antique and the space badly planned, more radical improvements are needed.

FIRST STEPS
Look through manufacturers' brochures to find a style you like. Although many of the rooms shown are larger than the average family bathroom, there are plenty of good ideas on how fixtures can be arranged. Some manufacturers offer a free planning guide.

Specialists If you can, it is worth visiting some bath specialist shops where you will find tubs, lavatories and fixtures in many different shapes and colors. Specialists are a good source of non-standard size baths, such as steeping tubs. You'll also see unusual finishes, such as cultured marble and metallic effects. Some specialists sell shower stalls including the latest 'environmental enclosures,' complete with soft rain effect and piped music. Many specialists have a range of faucets, tiles, towels, flooring and accessories, so it is possible to do all your bathroom shopping under one roof.

Color choice When looking at brochures, remember that color printing can be deceptive. Most plumbingware manufacturers supply color samples that can be matched up with wallcoverings, flooring and tiles. Take the color sample with you when you shop and ask if you can compare colors in natural light – shop neon changes tones.

Plumbing If you are unsure how changes might affect plumbing – and whether or not restrictions would make your plans possible, ask a plumber for a survey.

Ventilation Lack of ventilation causes condensation in bathrooms. A vent fan ducted to the outside disposes of steam without bringing in cold air.

A ducted fan wafts steam out through ducting that travels between walls to the outside air.

STARTING FROM SCRATCH
Installing a brand new bathroom is an opportunity to get everything right. New fixtures, flooring, lighting, heating and decoration give you the chance to plan a room to suit both your tastes and your lifestyle. Use the checklist below to decide what you would like in your new bathroom before you make a plan and choose the fixtures.

Make a plan Measure the room and draw the shape of the room onto graph paper, allowing one big square per 10in. As well as the length, width and height of the room, mark the following on the plan:
☐ The size and location of the door and the direction in which it opens.
☐ Size, location and type of windows.
☐ Location of the hot and cold water supplies.
☐ Hot water heater location and capacity.
☐ Radiator or heated towel rail.
☐ Electrical outlets and switches.
☐ Anything you want to keep.

CHOOSING FIXTURES
Remodeling your bathroom does not necessarily mean buying new fixtures. If the existing suite is in good condition but badly placed, it may be worth moving it around. Alternatively, if you hate the color, think about having the tub and fixtures resurfaced. There are several specialist companies who offer this service. The work is done on site, there is a good choice of colors and the cost is about a quarter of the price of a new bathroom.

If your fixtures need replacement, look through manufacturers' brochures and make a list of products that appeal to your tastes. If the house is modern in style, concentrate on the new soft, clean pastels. If you live in a period home, look at Victorian style and decorated suites.

Before you make the final plan, it is important to note the fixture locations, the space around them and the best way to position them.

Plumbing The toilet needs to be connected to the main stack, (the big pipe which goes down to the main waste line.) Moving this is very difficult, so try to keep the toilet in the same place.

It is cost-effective to have the toilet, bidet, lavatory and tub in a line, so that there is one straight run of water pipes. The pipes can be concealed in a knee wall partition. It may be possible to position the partition across the room so it makes a low knee wall. Position the tub on one side and the toilet, lavatory and bidet on the other.

BATHROOM CHECKLIST
Before you buy any sort of bathroom equipment, list what is wrong with the current room, and what you would like to have.

☐ **Facilities** How many bathrooms, showers and toilets do you need? If the kids have left home, would you be better off with a master bedroom and bath suite, and a separate shower and toilet?

☐ **Location** Is your present bathroom in the right location?

☐ **Hot water** Does your present system provide enough hot water?

☐ **Who uses the bathroom?** Do you need to make safety provisions for elderly people or children?

☐ **The fixtures** Are they in good condition or do they need replacing?

☐ **Your budget** How much can you afford to spend?

☐ **Heating** Is the bathroom warm?

☐ **Ventilation** Does the bathroom suffer from condensation?

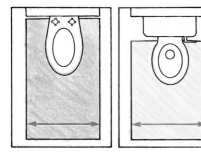

△ **Toilet and bidet space**
There should be enough space around the toilet and bidet for comfortable use – about 30in. wide and 42in. space in front.

Space around fixtures Sufficient floor space around fixtures is important if the bathroom is to work efficiently. There should be enough space around each item for it to be used comfortably. At the side of the tub, allow room for the user to get in and out easily and dry himself in comfort. A standing area 30in. wide at the side of the tub is the minimum comfortable space.

Space at the front and sides of the lavatory, toilet and bidet is equally important. Allow an area 30in. wide and 42in. long in front of the lavatory. Don't position a shelf or cupboard over the basin where someone could bump their head. The toilet and bidet should be set in an area about 30in. wide with 42in. of space in front. If the toilet and bidet are side-by-side, the space between them can be decreased as it is unlikely that both will be used at the same time.

If the bathroom has a separate shower stall, make sure the entrance is not obstructed and that there is enough space for the door to open fully. If

▽ **Build a plumbing wall**
If you site the lavatory, tub, bidet and toilet along one wall, piping can be hidden in a duct. Shaded areas show the space needed for fixtures.

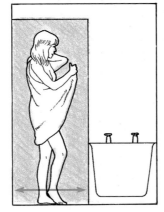

△ **Beside the tub**
Allow enough space (30in. minimum) beside the bath for users to climb in and out and to dry themselves.

△ **Around the lavatory**
Space around the lavatory is important, allow 30in. wide and 42in. in front. Avoid deep shelves above lavatory.

space is limited, choose an enclosure with a sliding door. Allow about 30in. of standing space in front of the shower.

POSITIONING FIXTURES
The way fixtures are positioned can help to make your bathroom practical and pleasant to use.

The bath The usual site for the tub is with one side and one or both ends hard up against a wall, but if space and plumbing permit, it is possible to achieve a more interesting layout by centering the bath along a wall, or in the middle of the floor.

If the tub is positioned with the side centered in the middle of a long wall, you can build a plumbing partition duct along the faucet end and place the lavatory or toilet on the other side of it. The plumbing wall should end at about 30in. above the floor. The space above can be left open, or can be filled with shelving or a display of plants. The advantage of doing this is that the tub is screened from the rest of the room, so more than one person can use the facilities at a time.

Another idea is to build a floor-to-ceiling tiled partition at each end of the tub so that it is enclosed in an alcove. Put the toilet at one end and a shower stall at the other.

The lavatory If there is space, install two to ease the strain on the bathroom at peak times. Make sure that there is enough space for two people to stand at the basins. If the toilet is in the bathroom, place the lavatory close by. Make sure, too, that there is a towel rack close to the lavatory and wall space for a toothbrush holder and soap dish.

Toilet and bidet Ideally, the toilet and bidet should be separate from the bathroom, but in many homes lack of space makes this impossible. You may have very little choice on position as it depends on the location of the main soil stack, but if possible, locate the toilet close to a window or ventilation. The bidet should be beside the toilet.

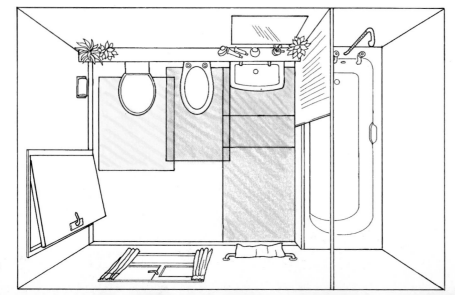

BATHROOMS FOR CHILDREN
☐ A step up to the tub makes climbing in and out easier.
☐ A shower stall fitted with a thermostatically controlled shower means that children can wash safely, unattended.
☐ As children have a habit of locking themselves in bathrooms, install a lock that can be opened with a screwdriver from the outside.
☐ A plastic box on wheels makes a good home for bathtime toys.
☐ Install a locking cupboard for medicine.

THE PERFECT BATHROOM

Ideas to help you turn your bathroom from the plainly functional to the handsomely designed.

The bathroom is where we start and end the day, and the bleak discomfort of a cheerless room is not an inviting prospect. Until recently, bathroom design tended towards the utilitarian. Most of the bathrooms contained little more than the basic tub, lavatory and toilet, with perhaps a medicine cabinet and a few shelves. At last bathrooms are receiving the attention enjoyed by other areas of the home.

In the built-in bathroom the familiar trio of tub, lavatory and toilet can be linked with a continuous run of units, providing sleek surfaces and cupboards sealed against moisture. Systems can start with a simple vanity unit and build up to wall units, corner cupboards and open and closed shelving.

A built-in bathroom can look handsome. Accessory clutter is tidied away and a clean line given to what is often a cumbersome array of plumbingware. You can add finishing touches to pro-

vide a pleasant room to relax in – even a comfortable chair, if there's space.

If you live in an older house with a generous-size bathroom, you could plan more ambitiously. Perhaps include a dressing area or, in these health-conscious days, have a workout section. Think about installing laundry facilities, to deal with the used laundry where it generates. Remember, though, to comply with safety regulations – get expert advice before installing electrical appliances.

Even if you haven't space for lavish projects, modern fixtures can transform a spartan bathroom into a room that's a delight to use.

Storage style
A bathroom that looks fresh and inviting has been designed to make use of all available space. Glass doors allow a collection of pretty objects to be displayed, while less sightly objects are stowed neatly behind mirrored doors, wooden cabinets and inside drawers.

◁ *Elegant style*
This beautiful mahogany vanity is crafted in an adaptation of the Adam brothers' style from the late 18th century. A piece such as this creates a degree of elegance for the bathroom that is usually only found in the rest of the home. Behind the mahogany doors, which have a swirl pattern and strip mahogany border, are practical pull-out storage trays.

▽ *Beech bathroom*
These handsome wall-hung units would suit all but the tiniest of rooms, and the warm beech and white finish looks crisply trim and stylish. Bathroom requisites can be stored in cupboards and drawers, and open shelving gives easy access to towels and toiletries.

BATHROOM BASICS

Before you start considering a choice of units, work out your plans based on the size and shape of your room: will your budget and space stretch to a full range of built-in units? Will sleek lines look out of place in an older-style or traditionally furnished house?

A built-in bathroom needn't be brutally modern: many traditional-style units are available. Materials are the same as those used for built-in kitchens – colored laminated plastics, various wood finishes and some luxury manmade or natural materials. Whatever the finish, rounded edges and corners are essential for safety and comfort.

The fullest range of built-in bathrooms extends to a wide choice of storage cabinetry – full height, low level, or high level – to house everything that gathers in a bathroom. Plumbing should be housed out of view, but be sure to provide access panels. Tub, lavatory and toilet tank can be encased, and work surfaces and shelving may be built-in.

Off-the-rack systems would suit a bathroom of standard proportions. Though more expensive, a custom-made line will give flexibility and make the most of valuable space.

If your bathroom is tiny, planning of every precious inch is essential. Consider a basic system of a small vanity unit with storage above and below, and plan wall units or shelving as space permits.

△ **Wall unit**
In this bathroom, one entire wall has been dedicated to a variety of sea-green storage units. A circular shower with adjoining whirlpool bath is a contemporary luxury.

▽ **Bathroom cheer**
A modern version of a vanity unit provides neat storage under double basins. Note how the accessories have been carefully selected to match the stylish red trim.

◁ *Television craze*
It is not unusual these days to find a built-in space for a TV set; however, this bathroom provides space for two! Clean towels are only an arm's length away when stored in the handy cubbyhole. A shelf with family photographs and special art pieces give the room a personal touch.

▽ *Practically pretty*
Another design that makes the most of all the available space, with high- and low-level storage. Even the toilet tank housing is incorporated into the work-surface run, with adjacent cupboard storage in an area that is not normally put to efficient use.

A PLACE FOR EVERYTHING

Once you've decided on the main units, you will have to plan efficient use of the storage space. Make a list of all the items you need to store – this will include necessities such as stocks of toilet paper, soap and shampoo, and cleaning materials. You also need to find space for extra towels, bathrobes and perhaps linen as well as storage for used laundry. Toiletries, cosmetics and medicine all need allotted space.

If this is your only bathroom, you will need to arrange handy storage of essentials needed for peak-time family use. How often is a particular item used? For example, if you store fresh supplies of baby's diapers in the bathroom they must be readily accessible.

One of the pleasures of a built-in bathroom is that you can tuck away all the less sightly necessities like bathroom cleaners and toilet paper. Extra towels can also be stored in closed cupboards. Medicine should be housed beyond the reach of children in a special cabinet with a lock or safety catch.

Reserve open storage – shelves and work surfaces – for items that look good, like pretty toiletries and plants that thrive in a moist atmosphere. Make sure, though, that you don't cram in too much to spoil the streamlined look of your built-in bathroom.

▷ Some light reading
A large bathroom can serve a dual purpose. Here, large bookshelves finished in faux marble provide space for a wall of books. The elaborate style of this salon, featuring marble floors, polished brass fixtures and a floor-to-ceiling mirror, accentuates the wild-rose-colored fixtures.

▽ Richly wooden
Natural materials can add warmth to soften the functional aspects of a modern bathroom. These sturdily attractive high- and low-level pine units provide plenty of storage, and would be ideal if you wanted to give your bathroom a robust country air.

13

BATHROOM EXTRAS

Many modern bathroom cabinets are provided with internal fittings to give a clever selection of concealed laundry and garbage baskets, wire basket storage for towels, integral mirrors and lighting, and many other extras. Most of these have borrowed inspiration from the built-in kitchen, and an enterprising DIY expert could even adapt standard kitchen organizers for bathroom use.

Corner carousels can provide valuable storage in a tight corner. Trays are designed to swivel out so you don't have to delve deep into cupboards to forage for small items – an added convenience is that makeup can be used straight from the tray. Some storage ideas are very neat. Soap dishes can slide away after use to give a flush surface, and a few units even have a special built-in radio.

Though most bathroom accessories can be neatly stored, some essentials need to be left out for convenient use. Look for accessories that will complement your overall scheme, as you don't want to spoil the clean lines of a built-in bathroom with a hodgepodge of unmatched extras. Towels are generally very evident in a bathroom; choose them to match the overall scheme. Storage ideas range from wall-high heated ladders to small fitments designed to hold guest towels. Some manufacturers provide color-matched items such as bathroom cups and towel rings. For a streamlined effect, choose accessories such as soap dishes that are inset rather than projecting.

Built-in units often have integral lighting for tasks such as shaving. For applying makeup, consider Hollywood-style light bulbs set around a mirror for a touch of real glamour.

△ *Door detail*
This view of shelving set on the inside of a wall-unit door shows how much can be kept in a very little space. Larger items such as towels are stored in the cupboard itself, with smaller toiletries shelved inside the door.

△ *Tray hold-all*
Drawer space can be fitted with trays that will keep separate little items that are so easily mislaid. Here, cosmetics are stored ready for use straight from the tray.

△ *Bathroom carousel*
An idea originally developed for the kitchen that works equally well in the modern bathroom. Door-mounted swivel trays give immediate access to personal toiletries.

BRIGHT IDEA

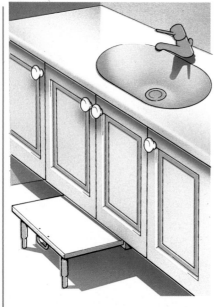

PLATFORM PERFORMANCE

Bathroom fixtures are developed with adults in mind; they often leave small children with an awkward stretch to reach lavatory and faucets.

This sturdy platform pulls out at washtime, and will help a child develop independence in the bathroom while still remaining safe. Once the child has finished, the platform slides beneath the wall-hung units to leave the way clear for other, taller, bathroom users.

Take care where you place chemicals and drugs. All medicines should of course be kept behind a child-proof door that is also well beyond a child's reach. Many bathroom units now incorporate a high-level medicine cabinet.

△ *Laundry storage*
The lower cupboard door of this unit swings open to allow easy disposal of used laundry. Clearing the floor space of freestanding items like laundry baskets leaves the room clutter-free.

MAKING THE MOST OF SMALL BATHROOMS

A small bathroom can be very cozy, but there's usually room for improvement.

Although catalogs from manufacturers of bathrooms illustrate larger-than-life settings, most of us have to deal with much smaller rooms.

THE OPTIONS

If the rest of your accommodation is generous, you can make a separate shower stall room or toilet, freeing valuable space and reducing pressure on the bathroom itself. Or, if a room next door is large enough, you can 'borrow' some of that space and enlarge your bathroom. These solutions, however, are expensive, involving both major plumbing and building expenses.

More realistically, you can try to work with what you have. In terms of rearranging the plumbing, it is relatively easy to change the position of the lavatory, more difficult to change the position of the tub, and hardest of all to move the toilet.

A cheaper alternative is to replace large, and perhaps outdated or ugly fixtures with smaller, more compact and modern ones.

The easiest and least expensive solution is to use color, pattern and mirrors to create an illusion of space.

High-level ideas Many small bathrooms are too high in proportion to their floor area. Transform some of this high-level space into storage: cupboards above the tub are one possibility; building a narrow shelf between the top of the door and the ceiling another. Or try continuing the ceiling color a short distance down the walls to the line of an imaginary picture rail to improve the proportions of the room.

Neat boxing in of any exposed plumbing work and clever conversion of awkward areas into concealed extra storage space will help to streamline a small room.

Cool and pretty

Crisp white paneling, fresh florals and pale blue tiles give an air of sophistication to this ordinary, rectangular bathroom. Notice how the baseboard has been continued around the bath panel and into the recess under the vanity unit. A pretty balloon shade in a charming flowery print disguises the frosted glass window; the same fabric is used for the chair cushion. A row of flower-pattern tiles, the houseplants and prints all echo the floral theme.

△ *Stunningly simple*
Palest pink fixtures with candy-striped tiles make the most of this elegant bathroom.

Clever positioning of two large sheets of mirrored glass opposite each other carry reflections to infinity and create the impression that the tub is set into an alcove. As there is no shower attachment, and the bath is set a tile's width in from the wall, shelves could be built above the end of the tub. These could be used for storing towels and other essentials.

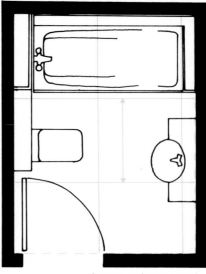

1 square = 1 square yard

▷ *Off the floor*
For a really sleek effect, wall-hung fixtures create a spare, uncluttered look (floor plan above).

There wasn't enough room for a separate shower, so one has been built into the wall at the end of the tub. The strongly patterned shower curtain coordinates with the wallpaper border. There are glass shelves above the built-in toilet tank while the solid shelf next to the lavatory has been tiled.

SMALL AND STYLISH
Used cleverly, mirrors can appear to double the size of a room, while the clean lines of modern, wall-hung fixtures, together with a sophisticated color scheme, will help to create a sense of space.

Reflections Bathroom mirrors have far greater potential than being used just for shaving or brushing your teeth.

Mirror tiles come in all sizes, from tiny mosaic squares to huge glass panels, and range from the traditional silver to smokey gray and warm, pink-tinged tones. Tinted mirrors and small mirror tiles are kinder to less-than-perfect naked bodies than large panels of silvered mirrors.

In poorly ventilated bathrooms, condensation on mirrors can be a problem,

BRIGHT IDEA

Double shower curtain If you want to use a shower curtain but can't find a ready-made one to go with your color scheme, use a coordinating fabric. Punch holes in the fabric, reinforce them, and clip on plastic rings to attach a waterproof lining.

and glass mirror tiles feel cold to the touch. Acrylic mirrors and tiles are slightly better in this respect and are lighter in weight but are easily scratched. Make sure any mirror you buy is suitable for bathroom use, or the mirrored backing may come off.

Like ceramic tiles, mirror tiles need to be attached to rigid, even surfaces, and large mirrors require sound walls.

Fixture solutions Whether creating a new bathroom or replacing existing units, remember that wall-hung lavatories and toilets take less floor space than conventionally supported bathroom fixtures and that cleaning under them is simple. Be careful of weak internal walls; lavatories weigh least, but an occupied toilet is very heavy. If in doubt, consult a reputable builder or designer.

Although there are no scaled-down toilets, there are models with slim-line tanks, ideal for ducting. There are also small lavatories, usually advertised as being suitable for small master bathrooms, but equally useful in tiny bathrooms. These may be too small to be useful for anything other than washing hands. Manufacturers offer a range of shapes and colors to fit your style.

◁ *Tiling interest*
An interesting pastel scheme gives a spacious feel to a small room. Woodwork and tiling are in the same gray and are a contrast to the pale pink walls. Tiling interest comes from the diamond pattern, which is continued around the mirror, creating a border.

▽ *Streamlined unity*
A narrow bathroom with a period feel is fitted into an area no more than 9ft. × 6½ft. The vanity unit has roomy cupboard space and the boxing in around the toilet tank is continued up to the ceiling to make open-shelved storage.

The uncluttered feel is created by building in the bath and the lavatory in a continuous line, matching up the line of the baseboard with the bottom of the paneled fixtures.

CLEVERLY CONCEALED

The smaller the bathroom, the more important it is that dull or unattractive items are kept out of sight.

If you are replacing bathroom fixtures, go for the sleekest ones you can find – products that have been designed so that the plumbing can be concealed or ducted. Alternatively, you can combine clean lines with hidden storage space by building in your fixtures.

If the toilet and lavatory follow one wall, and the supply and waste pipes are laid in a single line, the whole lot, including a slim-line toilet tank, can be hidden behind a specially built false wall, finished to match the scheme of the bathroom. The top of the wall can be used as a narrow shelf for accessories or ornaments. (Make sure you can open a panel to gain access to the pipes and tank.)

Storage If the tank is on a long wall, boxing it in could include shelving on either side or above.

Boxing in the lavatory is a smaller scale project, and there are ready-made vanity units available from manufacturers. If the front has a door, you will have the perfect hideaway for shampoo bottles, cleaning materials and spare toiletries.

TIGHT ON SPACE

If you have a really small bathroom, perhaps where you have 'borrowed' space to make a master bathroom, you may not have the room to fit in a conventional tub.

The obvious answer is a shower but, for those who prefer a bath, a sit-down model provides an up-to-the-neck soak. In the room on the right, this arrangement gives you a tub, toilet and lavatory without overcrowding.

To avoid a small room's becoming claustrophobic, keep color schemes simple – go for clean lines, either with light, neutral backgrounds to create a sense of space, or choose a single clear color for a brighter effect. This is not the place for unnecessary clutter, so keep it all out of sight; built-in storage is a definite bonus in this situation.

A real plus in a small bathroom is that you can splurge on a few more expensive materials than usual – tiles, fabrics and flooring – without breaking the bank.

1 square = 1 square yard

△ **Deep water**
Where there is no space for a conventional tub, consider a sit-down model. Using pale wall and floor tiles gives a quiet, restful mood to this very small room. The neutral scheme also helps blur the boundaries between the floor, wall and sides of the tub, creating a sense of space.

◁ **Mellow yellow**
The alternative solution is a shower stall (floor plan above). This time the color scheme is simple but stunning – all white fixtures and tiles in the shower contrasted with bright yellow vinyl wallpaper, rubber flooring and accessories. A corner opening shower door is the best choice for this tight space.

◁ Country look

This bathroom in an older house has been given a country feel by taking easily cleaned gloss-painted tongue-and-groove boarding up to the windowsill level. This is higher than a normal dado rail but is very practical in a bathroom. The bath has been set 6in. in from the window wall, thus creating a useful shelf.

The 'dead area' above the toilet is taken up with a roomy cabinet, painted to match the wainscoting with a door panel covered in the same paper as the walls.

A wide and wonderful wallpaper border defines the perimeters of the room and outlines the fairly small window.

△ Hidden storage

Sliding mirrored cabinets not only double the apparent size of this compact room, but give plenty of storage space. This very neat solution does, however, have a snag; the mirrors really must be kept immaculate or the whole effect is ruined. There is a special liquid available that can be applied to mirrors to help minimize misting in a steamy bathroom.

◁ Flower gardens

Delicately painted fixtures in the bathroom add warmth and style. This collection includes ceramic tile, faucet trim and countertop accessories that match the pedestal lavatory and toilet designs. A profusion of pink, blue and yellow blossoms and green tendrils reach out from areas of dense coloration onto the white background.

NEW LOOKS FOR OLD BATHROOMS

If you are not happy with the way your bathroom looks, think about how you can make it more stylish.

If your existing bathroom is looking tired and outdated, it is not difficult to improve on what you have. Even if you find it is too small for your family's needs there are ways around the problem.

Better use of space Rearranging the fixtures can make a surprising difference to the usable area, particularly if you rehang a door that opens into the center of the room so that it opens back against a wall. If the existing layout is really not making the best use of the available space, it is obviously well worth replacing the fixtures at the same time as relocating them. Experiment with squared paper and cutouts of your tub, lavatory and so on to find the best arrangement.

If a new layout is not viable, one answer could be to combine a bathroom and next-door toilet. This larger space may allow you to include two lavatories and/or a shower stall to help with the morning rush.

Other possibilities are to take in an adjacent hallway to make a bigger bathroom or to take some space from a next-door bedroom by moving the dividing wall.

An extra bathroom If you have one large bedroom, it might be a better plan to sacrifice part of it to make a small master bathroom or shower stall to relieve pressure on the main bathroom.

New look

A dilapidated bathroom (right) can be revived simply by redecorating. Bringing the ceiling color a little way down the walls and covering the top of the window with a shade are both ways of visually lowering the ceiling.

A great transformation has taken place in a similar room (below). Large mirrors add a much needed illusion of space and actually do multiply the level of light in the room. The windowsill has been built up by two tile widths, the bath is placed under the window and a new vanity unit updates the old lavatory. Crisp white with blue tiles make the room light and airy.

△ *Austere original*
This rather grim bathroom is in desperate need of redecoration. Although the original roll-top tub has been painted and has lost its claw feet, and the tub faucets are beyond repair, most of the period fixtures are in good condition and suit their setting far better than modern ones.

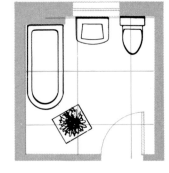

Scale: I square = I square yard

NEW VERSUS OLD

Before you start ripping out all your old bathroom fixtures and replacing them with brand new ones, look at them carefully. If they are in good condition you might only need to change the decoration – new tiling, paint and wallcovering and possibly some new faucets can be enough to effect a complete transformation.

You may find that your old tub is of better quality than most modern ones around today. Cast-iron tubs, for instance, were once commonplace but are now fairly difficult to find, as well as being expensive. If the only thing wrong with the tub is worn enamel or calcium deposits, it is possible to have it re-enameled.

When renovating older properties, many people go to great lengths to track down period bathroom faucets and fixtures that have been thrown out by remodelers. If you live in an old house, or would like to create a traditional bathroom, there are a growing number of architectural salvage companies who deal in all sorts of period fixtures and faucets. There are also many manufacturers of reproduction plumbingware, faucets and accessories.

◁ Authentic mood

Here, the atmosphere of the period has been recreated and the room given a homey coziness. The tub has been renovated and the floor and woodwork are coated with glossy mahogany varnish. Plain dark green tiles were chosen for the area below the dado rail, with an edging of hand-decorated green/brown/white ones.

The old-fashioned double faucets were salvaged to retain the authentic feeling.

▽ Modern setting

The same room adapts well to a more modern treatment. The outside of the tub is painted gray with a black-and-yellow stenciled border to match the painted dado. The same three colors are used for the vinyl tiled floor.

BRIGHT IDEA

Border design Make a border to match your own color scheme by painting the relief design of an anaglypta border wallcovering. On this geometric pattern the background was painted gray and the raised design was picked out in the same yellow as the walls. Make sure you use an oil-based paint to protect your hard work from condensation.

BATHROOM FACELIFTS

The largest part of revamping an existing bathroom is the expense of plumbing and new fixtures. If you inherit a bathroom where everything works perfectly but just doesn't suit your taste, there are ways of changing the whole mood of the room without having to start from scratch.

Using color and pattern Look at the colors of the fixtures and tiles or anything else you can't afford to change, and make that your starting point. A wallcovering that picks up one or more of these colors in a bold pattern can look stunning, especially if it is emphasized by curtains and accessories that match or coordinate.

Even if it's very small, there's no reason why the bathroom shouldn't have style. Rich, full-length curtains or a decorative Austrian blind brighten up the dullest windows.

A pastel-colored, mini-print wallcovering, especially if used on the ceiling as well as the walls, can visually extend a small or dark bathroom. If light colors are used for the flooring and curtains, too, the effect is increased.

The bathroom no longer has to be a plain, functional and rather cold place that you spend as little time in as possible. As long as it is heated adequately, it may only take the addition of a carpet or thick rugs for it to be really warm and cozy, and a comfortable chair or elegant window seat can make it a truly inviting room.

△ *Pretty in pink*
The plain white tiles and fixtures in this small bathroom made it feel rather cold and bleak.

The new owners left the tub and very useful vanity unit as they were. They papered the walls with a warm pink mini-print vinyl covering and hung matching curtain and blind. Keeping the soap and towels pink and adding the potted cyclamen provide the finishing touches.

◁ *Luxurious looks*
Instead of choosing pale or neutral colors to go with the strong blue fixtures and mustard tiles, a daring approach was adopted. Bold floral wallpaper in a yellow with blue among other accents brings the room alive. Matching fabric is used for the elegant upholstered seat in front of the window and for the full-length curtains caught back with a silk tie at below-sill level. The large print above the tub has the same colors used in different proportions to pull the whole look together.

△ *Beautiful countryside*
An expansive mural featuring the beautiful countryside helps to create elegance in this traditional bathroom. Delicate swan towels and a bathtub tray with small lamps are stylish decorative touches.

BRIGHT IDEA

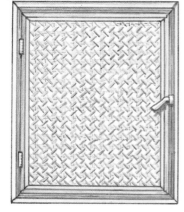

WAYS WITH WINDOWS
A boring frosted glass window or one that looks out on a dull view can be made more interesting.
☐ A sheet of caning cut to fit inside the window frame can be held in place against the glass with quarter-round beading.

☐ Glass shelves installed across a window look very attractive with a collection of small glass bottles or ornaments and potted plants standing on them.

Supported by slim brackets at either end, the shelves still allow some light to come through.

☐ As an alternative to net curtains or blinds, you can cover clear glass with self-adhesive vinyl made to look like stained glass for a period look.

It is easy to apply and easy to keep clean. Fairly small panes look best with this treatment.

QUICK CHANGE

The least expensive way to change the look of a bathroom is to add new accessories such as a matching mirror, toothbrush and mug holder and soap dish. Pale or neutral colored fixtures set against plain walls and floors are the most versatile.

In a white or cream room you can add a flowery balloon shade, pick out two or three of the colors for towels and add a wooden toilet seat and towel rail for a country look. Alternatively, choose a window shade with a strongly colored geometric design and take one color from this to use as an accent.

Stylish setting

A classic white suite, a black and white tiled floor and chrome fixtures are set against creamy walls (left). The look is spacious and smart but the mood is rather bleak.

The introduction of just one strong color – a blue-green – immediately makes this a more interesting scheme (below). The chrome trolley, mirrors and the pictures well-placed over the lavatories and tub further improve it. A couple of dramatic plants are the perfect finishing touch.

UNUSUAL BATHROOMS

A special bathroom can be created through the decoration or the shape and style of the tub itself.

A large bathroom, or one which is an odd shape, offers almost unlimited scope for creating an unusual atmosphere. But even a small, rectangular bathroom can, with a little ingenuity, be turned into something out of the ordinary. And an unexciting bathroom can be totally transformed if it is imaginatively combined with out-of-the-ordinary patterns and materials.

The fixtures, too, can transform a bathroom. The traditional materials for tubs – cast iron and steel – are rigid, stable and durable as well as cold to the touch and extremely heavy. Modern materials are not only lighter in weight and warmer to the touch, they are also easily molded – making it possible to incorporate backrests, seats and even inset soap trays. Hence the modern generation of tubs, many of which are a far cry from standard traditional rectangular shapes.

Corner tubs, round tubs, and sit-in tubs all look, and feel, distinctive. Whirlpool baths have the added bonus of providing gentle underwater massage in addition to a warm soak. Tubs that reproduce the elegance of the Victorian and Edwardian eras are increasingly widely available.

Finally, of course, you may want to choose a non-standard tub for practical as well as decorative reasons – to fit into a small space or make use of an odd angle, perhaps.

Tub addition
A medium-size bathroom becomes exceptional with the addition of a curved glass enclosure and glass-block wall. Light can enter from all angles, while retaining privacy for the bather.

◁ **Richly paneled**
Wood paneling on the tub, vanity unit and drawers produces a warm, unfussy atmosphere. The tongue-and-groove paneling on the walls has been laid diagonally, with alternating light and dark panels, to create added interest in what could otherwise become a rather dark expanse of wood.

▷ **Conservatory style**
For an exotic look, you can't beat a round tub! Where there isn't space for a round tub in the center of the room, the tub can be positioned along a wall using angled panels. The floorcovering has been extended to cover the tub surround, for an uninterrupted look.

▽ **Flowery coordination**
Many period-style tubs are supplied unfinished on the outside. This means that you can simply paint the tub with gloss or semi-gloss paint in the color of your choice – or you can try more adventurous techniques such as rag rolling, dragging or stenciling. These charming sprays of flowers were handpainted to match the wallpaper.

STYLISH TUBS

Not all tubs are rectangular – many interesting shapes and sizes are available as part of manufacturers' standard lines. So finding a tub that meets your special requirements should pose no problems.

The simplest variations differ little from the common rectangular shape. Shorter-than-usual tubs are available to fit into smaller-than-usual rooms – and there are also extra-long tubs for tall people. Contoured tubs, which are waisted in the middle, tracing the outline of the human body, are both comfortable and economical on water.

Corner tubs not only look different, they can also be extremely practical. Many have a built-in shelf or ledge – ideal for sitting children on or resting your novel or magazine safely out of the water. Since the sides of the smallest corner tub are 48in. in length (considerably shorter than the conventional 60in. to 66in.), they are particularly suited to small or irregularly shaped bathrooms.

Round tubs provide a taste of 'Hollywood-style' bathing, but also require a 'Hollywood-size' bathroom to create the desired effect!

Whirlpool tubs are also known as spa baths or Jacuzzis. Nozzles in the sides of the bath pump out pressurized streams of water to massage as well as cleanse.

Sit-in tubs are square and squat in shape, ideal where space really is in short supply.

Period tubs incorporate the elegant details of Victorian and Edwardian designs – fluted or scalloped edges, decorative patterns, brass faucets and accessories. They also take advantage of up-to-date materials and technology. Modern conveniences such as bidets as well as tubs and lavatories are available.

Some period tubs are freestanding with ball and claw legs; others are elegantly enclosed in wooden paneling. Lavatories are frequently inset into wooden washstands or vanity units. Toilets often have wooden seats.

A touch of flamboyance To locate a really special tub, consult one of the growing number of bathroom specialists, where you might find a striking heart-shaped or hexagonal tub – or even a tub for two!

BRIGHT IDEA

A ceramic bath mat can be worked into the floor of even a small bathroom. Different combinations of colored tiles are set in a pattern, forming a rectangular (or any other shape) ceramic bath mat. Even the most ordinary bathrooms become colorful and exciting with creative tiling.

A TOUCH OF LUXURY

You may eventually tire of fancy bathroom fixtures that at first seem stunning, so it's often best to stick to something fairly simple, and splurge on the decoration instead. Repainting a wall is cheaper than buying a new tub!

Since the bathroom is a private place, and you don't actually live in the room, colors, patterns and styles that you couldn't tolerate elsewhere in the home can be used to good effect. (Don't get too carried away: check that the materials you want to use can resist heat, moisture and steam.) Lighting can reinforce the atmosphere – bright lights for a high-tech effect or glowing lighting for something more intimate.

Also consider the positioning of the fixtures – a tub at right angles to the wall can make an interesting focal point. Similarly, an ordinary tub can be transformed if the surround is fully tiled, paneled, or carpeted. A sunken tub invokes a feeling of luxury – and if you can't sink the tub into the floor, build up the floor instead.

△ *Inviting oasis*
The bathroom is the perfect place to create a daring decorating style. The opulent marble used for the walls and floor of this room emits a feeling of privacy as well as luxury.

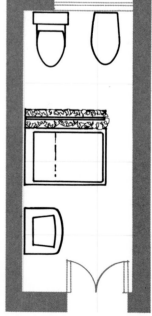

△ *Making space*
In order to squeeze all the fixtures into a small bathroom, it is often necessary to make compromises. To free space in this long, narrow bathroom for a bidet as well as a tub, toilet and lavatory, the original standard-size tub was replaced by a much smaller sit-in tub. A half-height wall was then constructed in order to screen off the tub from the toilet and bidet.

Scale: I square = I square yard

▷ **A second bathroom**
If you would like to add an extra bathroom to your home but haven't enough space for a standard tub, a small tub may answer your problem. Extra-short tubs are available that can be under 40in. long. They are ideal for children and perfectly adequate for occasional use by visitors.

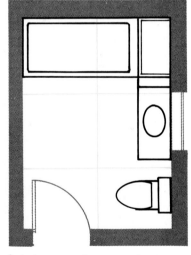

Scale: I square = I square yard

◁ **Adding a shower**
Since a small tub makes a good base for a shower, a brass shower head has been installed. The shower curtain, hung from a brass shower rod to match the faucets, keeps the rest of the room free from splashes.

Patterned tiles look attractive in a small room so long as they are part of a complete color scheme – here they coordinate with the blue and white of the side panels of the tub.

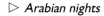
▷ Arabian nights

This fantasy bath employs an Arabian Nights theme to suggest luxury and seclusion, key elements in today's dream bathroom. A cream-colored whirlpool bath is enhanced with polished gold faucets, while the matching lavatory is set in a mirrored vanity. Recessed lighting provides a cool, romantic glow.

The paisley fabric, reminiscent of a Persian carpet, covers the walls and soffits. Lavish use of draped fabric at the entrance of the room and on the windows and ceilings suggests a tent billowing in the desert. The result is a glamorous, ultra-private room.

◁ Extravaganza in pink and blue

A little imagination and a lot of courage can create a dream-like environment in an ordinary, rectangular bathroom with standard fixtures.

The walls have been divided into three zones. The lowest section visually links the tub and lavatory. The middle blue section is splattered with pink and two shades of blue, linking the blue of the floor and the ceiling. Finally, the uppermost section (above a narrow glass shelf) is painted dusky pink to match both the beading around the tub and the pattern in the blue section of the wall. The gleaming bathroom fixtures add a crisp note and reflect the surrounding colors.

An arched, recessed mirror turns the lavatory into a striking feature, and carefully chosen accessories add the finishing touches to this very individual bathroom.

BATHROOM SURFACES

Surfaces need to be practical as well as attractive to survive the extreme conditions in a bathroom.

Extreme temperatures, steam and moisture all take their toll on a bathroom surprisingly quickly. Surfaces need to be tough, waterproof and easy to maintain if they are to survive bathroom conditions and look good.

The most common materials are paint, wallcovering, tiles, or a combination. The colder, harder and shinier the surface, the more it will suffer from condensation. Mirrors and windows are the first to mist up and steam will turn quickly to water against a tiled wall.

CONDENSATION

Unless a bathroom is kept warm and well-ventilated, moisture in the air from a steaming hot bath or shower condenses, streaming down the walls and misting up mirrors and windows. In a small bathroom or in one without a window, the problems are multiplied.

The two basic ways to deal with condensation are to install a ventilator and to keep the bathroom at a constant temperature.

Ventilation To stop the bathroom from misting up, it is essential to allow the moisture-laden air to escape. Fans that rely on convection should be positioned high on the outside wall, removing the warm, wet air as it rises. Power ventilators are more efficient, sucking the moist air out.

Warmth There are several kinds of auxiliary heaters if you don't have central heating or want to boost the temperature during the winter; wall-fixed fan heaters or portable heaters warm up a room quickly and, although inadequate on its own, a heated towel bar gives some background heat.

White practicality

Wall-to-ceiling tiling is, perhaps, the ultimate answer to the need for a waterproof and washable environment. Here, not only the walls but also the tub and lavatory surrounds are covered in classic white tiles. Red detail and a scarlet vinyl floor break up the otherwise stark and shining whiteness.

WALLCOVERINGS

Wallpapers, vinyl and foil wallcoverings are perfectly suitable for bathrooms, and patterns are great disguisers of uneven surfaces.

Wallcoverings require a sound smooth surface that has been well prepared and sized before they are hung. For best results, always use a fungicidal adhesive. Wallcovering can absorb a small amount of moisture but in really damp conditions it may start to peel and curl at the edges and joins, although sealants are available which provide a clear protective coat. Always test a sealant on a small area first to check that your paper is colorfast.

Although washable wallcovering can-

not withstand repeated scrubbing, it can be washed down fairly vigorously.

Vinyl is more expensive than ordinary wallcovering, but more robust due to the layer of vinyl fused onto a stout paper backing. It is also tough and moisture-resistant.

Plain textured vinyls can be used to simulate those fabric coverings that would be unsuitable in a bathroom – silk, hessian, grass-cloth, for example. Others convincingly mimic the look of ceramic tiles at less cost; they are also warmer to the touch than ceramic.

Foil wallcoverings are steam-resistant and highly light-reflective, making them excellent for dark rooms that don't get much sunlight.

▷ *Opulent looks*

An attic bathroom can appear cramped but this one looks good and is also practical.

Most of the available surfaces, including the vented cupboard doors, are covered in a mini-print paper, offset by patterned tiles that protect the backsplash areas around the tub and between the lavatory and mirror. Bold floral curtains on either side of the tub give extra height to the sloping ceiling.

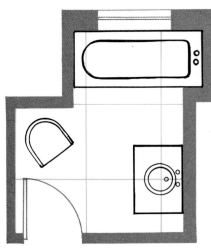

◁ **Seaside theme**
The walls in this pale bathroom are covered in a practical vinyl wallpaper, resilient enough to withstand splashes and drips. The woodwork is painted in white gloss and the tub panel is covered in matching wallpaper protected by a coat of clear polyurethane.

▷ **Pastel alternative**
A different vinyl wallcovering is the basis for this ice-cream colored scheme. Pale pink tiles in the alcove around the shower, under the window and behind the lavatory make a practical backsplash. Wooden panels, painted pink, blue and green, are fitted along the tub and under the lavatory.

PAINT

The cheapest and easiest way to decorate bathroom walls is to paint them with an oil-based paint, either satin or semi-gloss. Gloss is not advisable on walls as it tends to highlight the effects of condensation, can cause glare, and reveals imperfections on uneven wall surfaces. Latex is easy to apply and is a good disguiser of surface defects but is not so easy to wash.

Traditional paint effects such as sponging, rag-rolling and marbling work well in bathrooms. The durable colored glazes used in many of these techniques make them particularly suitable for steamy environments.

TILING

Glazed ceramic wall tiles are the most practical work surface of all and can be used from floor to ceiling, up to dado height, or just around splash areas. Tiling a whole room can be costly, but it is a one-time investment that is usually worthwhile in terms of durability.

The variety of patterns, sizes, colors and textures available has largely dispelled the cold and clinical image of tiles, and there are prices to suit most budgets. Tiling a bathroom is a straightforward job and, if you are a DIY enthusiast, one that you can do yourself.

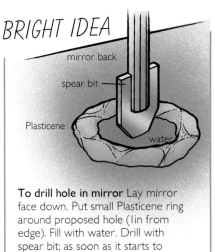

mirror back

spear bit

Plasticene

water

To drill hole in mirror Lay mirror face down. Put small Plasticene ring around proposed hole (1in from edge). Fill with water. Drill with spear bit; as soon as it starts to break through, turn over and finish hole from front.

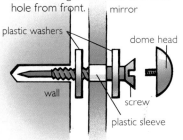

plastic washers

mirror

dome head

wall

screw

plastic sleeve

Install mirror Use screws with dome covers. Fit plastic washers either side of mirror. Protect hole with plastic sleeve. Don't overtighten screws to avoid cracking mirror.

△ *Totally tiled*
The white tiled floor and walls and large mirror by the tub are a good choice in this small, high-ceilinged bathroom. The hard effect is softened with plants, shells and fluffy towels.

Plain or patterned tiles can be used equally as well in a modern or, as here, a more old-fashioned bathroom.

◁ *Special effects*
The opportunities are unlimited when it comes to painted tiles. The tiles in this room are painted in such a way that large vases of flowers, singing birds and vine-covered columns come alive. The lavatory coordinates with the yellow and blue border. An earthen-red floor adds to the color scheme.

▷ *Roman garden*
Step up to this sunken tub and walk into a Roman garden. A painted mural, which surrounds the tub, features a bird bath and a Roman landscape. Other Roman touches include a carved stone bench and a shiny faucet in the shape of a fish.

▷ *Granite top*
With its long-lasting moisture resistance, and its natural beauty, stone is an excellent material for use in the bathroom. Here, a granite countertop surrounds the lavatory. White surfacing materials were used to create a feeling of spaciousness. To enhance this, wall heights were varied and decorative ledges added.

◁ *Zigzag*
A tiled wall next to the tub makes practical sense. The colors in this contemporary interpretation of a wall mosaic are repeated throughout the room. A rose-pink-colored tub, matching mini blinds, a green soap dish, a neutral-colored tub surround and a towel of each color creates a unified feeling.

BATHROOM FLOORS

Aesthetics combine with the practical to produce a multitude of flooring materials suitable for bathrooms.

For most people, choosing a bathroom floor is first and foremost a practical concern. It will get splashed, it must not be slippery when wet, and it must be easy to keep clean. These factors are still more important when it comes to family bathrooms, or those used by young children or the elderly – bathroom fixtures are, by nature, solid and angular, and will not make for a soft landing should you slip. Bathroom floors are defined as being hard or soft, and a multitude of designs and surface finishes fall into these two categories. So, though for most people practical and safety considerations play an important role, don't neglect the aesthetic qualities of the various flooring materials.

Hard floors include marble tiles and slabs, terra-cotta and ceramic tiles. Un-glazed tiles and those with a non-slip finish or textured surface are especially suitable. Wood flooring can be polished, varnished, painted, or poly-urethaned, though the last two finishes are easier to maintain; polished floor-boards will mark when they are splashed with water, leaving white stains.

Resilient flooring – rubber and a variety of vinyls – are all versatile, dur-able and easy to maintain, provided you choose a reputable make. If you choose rubber, look at the textured finishes carefully: such a floor is obviously a sen-sible choice, but some rubber stud floorings are very bumpy, and cleaning around the studs is laborious. Vinyl flooring comes in tile and sheet form, and in many designs, patterns and colors. The most slip-resistant vinyl floors are contract quality, made for use in hospitals and other public buildings, where safety standards are very strictly regulated.

Soft finishes include cushioned vinyl and carpets. Though ordinary carpeting can be used, it is advisable to specify a bath-room quality carpet as this has a rub-berized backing and cotton or synthetic pile so it will not rot or get smelly when it gets wet. Remember, as well as a damp atmosphere and splashed water, bathroom carpets are sometimes sub-jected to a liberal dusting of talcum powder as well! In a small bathroom, therefore, it may be sensible to get a pastel-colored or patterned carpet that is machine washable for easy care and maintenance.

▽ *Marbled paradise*
If it's a rich design you are looking for, what could be more so than a room of marble? The surface is hard and colorful and filled with intricate patterns. However, marble stains easily and requires frequent waxing. Slabs are available in sizes up to 40 square feet and come in a range of colors. Here, the marble is continued up the walls and around the tub.

◁ **Tile solution**
Tiling is the common choice for a bathroom floor. One way to turn this ordinary solution into something extraordinary is to install a ceramic 'bath mat' next to the tub or shower stall (see Bright Idea, page 29). Here, the 'bath mat' gives a small bathroom a spacious, elongated feeling. A tiled tub surround and tiled wall with decorative border are practical, long-lasting effects.

◁ **Carpet for comfort**
This spacious master suite for two is a celebration of romance. Dusty rose and lavender tones are carried throughout the decorative wall fabric and faux-finish cabinetry. An exquisite oval stained-glass window, a pressed-tin ceiling, a roomy whirlpool for two and rose fretwork canopy reminiscent of a Victorian porch leave only one choice for the flooring: a plush wall-to-wall carpet in dusty rose. The carpeting will last longer if bath mats are used next to showers and tubs.

▷ **Period piece**
An elegant and old-fashioned cast-iron tub with ornate legs dominates this bathroom. A handpainted stenciled design runs around the tub, and the same gentle greens are used in the ceramic tiles, the armchair and the painted designs on the floor.

The floor is made up of plywood tiles, prepared and painted white before being stenciled in green and pink. Although stenciled floors take a certain amount of time and planning, you are guaranteed a highly individual result. Several coats of a high-gloss varnish were applied to seal the floor. Green and white wall tiles have been fixed diagonally and have been finished with stylish leafy tiles and curved ceramic bullnosed tiles.

▷ *Japanese style*
Narrow floorboards have been painted with black gloss paint and then varnished to create a hard-wearing and durable floor. The same approach is apparent throughout the bathroom, from the screens that frame the sunken tub to the kimono displayed opposite the tub. The streamlined built-in storage units incorporate the lavatory and ensure that the bathroom is kept relatively uncluttered.

▽ *Resilient floors*
Resilient floorcoverings, such as the one shown here, are especially good in rooms prone to splashes and spills. Durable, easily maintained and attractively designed, the new resilient floorcoverings wear longer and are available in a variety of appealing colors and patterns. Some even mimic natural materials such as marble, brick and clay. This versatility allows for many of the same choices as customized flooring. Look for floors with never-wax surfaces.

AROUND THE LAVATORY

Consider the area around the lavatory carefully when choosing bathroom fixtures, storage and accessories.

The lavatory and its surroundings are the functional heart of the bathroom. It's here that most activities – from making up to shaving – take place, so it follows that most equipment and accessories are necessarily grouped around the lavatory. Storage, lighting, a mirror and so on must all be provided.

As always, it is best to plan ahead: don't be tempted into buying an eye-catching item on impulse. Bathroom furniture and accessories come in a vast array of styles, colors and materials; shop around in order to assemble a personal selection.

Do you want a built-in look, with streamlined, built-in cupboards offering a maximum amount of hidden storage? Or would you prefer to keep more of your toiletries on display, and within easy reach when needed? Would traditional or modern fixtures be most in keeping with the style of your bathroom? Should the colors be plain white, dark hardwood – or perhaps bright primaries?

Bathroom furniture and accessories can be made from wood or plastic lam-inate; accessories are also available in chrome, china and porcelain.

Honey-colored pine or dark hardwood is warm to the touch; sealed with a polyurethane varnish, wood can resist the damage inflicted by heat and steam.

Laminates are ideal for bathroom use since they are hardwearing, easy to clean and come in bright colors, delicate shades and various textures.

Chrome accessories, which were particularly popular in the 1920s and 1930s, complement the chrome faucets that are still commonly found in today's bathrooms. And brass creates a luxurious effect. For a prettier, less masculine look, choose china or porcelain, which is often decorated with delicate flowers or birds. Be careful, though – china is easy to break or chip.

Built-in elegance
The sleek lines of built-in bathroom units combine open shelving and closed cabinets. Lights above the lavatory provide excellent task lighting – and elegant wooden rails on either side keep towels close at hand.

△ *Double vanity*
The double vanity is the focal point in this bathroom. Sitting on top of wooden cabinets, each lavatory is surrounded by sand-colored tiles.

◁ *In a niche*
The niche on the side wall provides space for the lavatory, a large mirror and sufficient storage. A dusty pink color brightens this useful corner.

THE CUSTOM LOOK

As well as making the best possible use of the usually limited space available in many modern bathrooms, custom cabinetry also creates clean, simple lines and banishes a great deal of clutter. A bathroom can incorporate as many built-in cabinets as a custom kitchen – a more modest built-in bathroom need include no more than a single wall-mounted unit.

The most basic custom furniture is a cabinet below the lavatory to utilize the normally wasted space beneath. Vanity units that fit around the lavatory, and wall-hung bathroom cabinets are available in many different sizes and styles. Look for versions that include extras such as a mirrored door, electrical outlet and light fixture.

SHAVING MIRROR

Where possible, a mirror should be hung above a lavatory, ideally so that you can see yourself from the back as well as the front. One way to achieve this is to hang an extendable shaving mirror next to another mirror so that it can be pulled out to reflect the view from behind.

A shaving mirror is also useful when a lavatory must be positioned below a window.

A word of caution: always check that the magnifying side of the shaving mirror faces away from fabrics to prevent them from scorching or even catching fire in strong sunlight.

△ **Tiled top**
A tiled countertop provides a long-lasting, easy-to-clean surface around the lavatories. The teal sinks have self-contained faucets.

▷ **White on white**
A stained-glass window, hung from the ceiling at the end of a double vanity unit, divides the bathroom into two separate areas.

STORAGE ON DISPLAY

Although a bathroom with plenty of built-in storage is easy to keep neat and tidy, it has the disadvantage of hiding all the personal bits and pieces that produce a lived-in feel. Today's toiletries are often so beautifully packaged that it is a pity to hide them away behind cabinet doors.

Open shelves allow cosmetics to be kept on hand. Although glass shelves look smart, they require frequent cleaning to remove grubby marks. Wood and laminate are both good alternatives. Stacking vegetable trays and plastic-coated shelves can be adapted for use in the bathroom; a cart on wheels can be pushed aside when not in use.

Cleaning materials and medicine are best kept out of sight; in a household that includes small children, they should be locked away behind a childproof lock. Consider installing a bathroom cabinet.

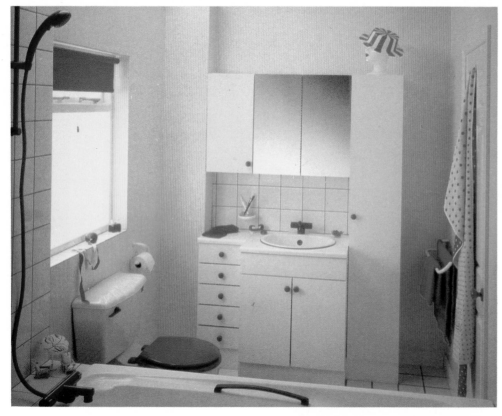

FINISHING TOUCHES

Whatever style you are aiming for in a bathroom, the finishing touches can make or break the effect. Look for coordinated accessories to complement the fixtures and decor.

Combined with white fixtures, carefully chosen accessories will themselves help to create the desired look. For example, a wooden clothes tree, a marble-topped washstand, brass faucets, and a mahogany toilet seat can set a Victorian-style bath scene.

Rather than replace a serviceable set of fixtures because you don't like its color or style, use accessories to transform the look of the room. If, for example, you have inherited avocado-colored fixtures, your first reaction may be to choose pale green towels and delicate china accents. Instead, try crisp navy and white accessories and use coral as an accent color.

Similarly, a primrose bathroom can be updated with a two-tone gray scheme: pale and charcoal gray towels with a striped blind and chrome toothbrush and toilet-paper holder.

△ ▷ *Color coordination*
To make it easier to achieve complete coordination in your bathroom, pick and choose items from a set of matching bathroom accessories. Most sets include the basics such as soap dishes, toilet-roll holders, towel racks, shelves, toothbrush holders, garbage and laundry baskets. Others also offer extras such as door and cabinet handles, faucets and shower attachments – even toilet seats.

In the bathroom pictured on the right, sunny yellow accessories add life to gray fixtures and white cabinets. Cherry red accessories make the almost identical bathroom shown above even livelier. In both cases, the wallcovering, colored grouting and matching window shades and towels complete the effect.

If you shop around, you should be able to find accessories in many colors – from the bright primaries shown in these two rooms to the natural wood, brass, and subtle pastels such as dusty pink and sage green illustrated below.

MASTER BATHROOMS

Add a touch of luxury and relieve pressure on family facilities with your own master bathroom.

The pressures on a family bathroom, particularly at peak times like the morning rush hour, can be considerable. In such circumstances, it would be a rare family that wouldn't welcome the addition of an extra bathroom. A bedroom with a master bathroom also adds a touch of luxury: it's good to be able to pamper yourself with your very own facilities, close to dressing and sleeping areas, and to enjoy the privacy of being able to move from one area to another without having to bother to put on clothes.

Planning ahead Installing a bathroom is expensive, but it should add value to your house unless you have to lose a bedroom in the process.

In a large home, with bedrooms surplus to normal family needs, replacing a small bedroom with an extra bathroom might well enhance the desirability of the property, as well as being of benefit to the current occupants. Otherwise it may be a better investment to spend a little more in the first place to achieve the optimum compromise of bedroom and bathroom.

To avoid losing a bedroom, consider moving a shared wall to take space from two adjoining bedrooms. If you have to reconcile yourself to positioning the new bathroom completely within your bedroom, there are several ingenious systems that provide bathroom facilities for tiny areas. Even a simple shower stall in a bedroom corner will help relieve the bathroom congestion.

It's important to get advice from a qualified plumber from the beginning. To keep down costs, make use of existing plumbing as far as you are able. Plumbing additions or alterations must comply with plumbing codes, and changes to the waste system have to conform to building codes: your local authority will be able to advise.

Master bath decor
With only a fireplace wall between them, the master bedroom and bathroom easily transfer from one to the next. The same styles are used in both rooms, including the sand-colored carpet which continues throughout both areas.

▽ **Cover story**
If you don't want jarringly functional equipment in the corner of a pretty bedroom, blend in the new installation by running wallpaper over cupboard doors as well as walls so that the bath merges smoothly into the bedroom scene. The lavatory here is a restful pastel shade; pink tones are emphasized in accessories.

INITIAL PLANNING

From the beginning you will need to take advice on the best positioning of plumbingware in relation to existing plumbing. Installing bulky equipment into a small space is quite a challenge, especially as you won't be able to move things once they're installed. Some manufacturers' brochures have cutout scale drawings of basic equipment, which you use with a plan to get an accurate idea of locations. Remember to leave enough space to use each facility in comfort and safety.

It's worthwhile ensuring everything, including labor, is the best you can afford. Poor installation could lead to dampness and condensation problems. **Ventilation** should be planned at the start. Opening a window could be drafty so consider instead an exhaust fan built into an exterior wall or window. If the new bathroom is completely internal, you *must* install a fan. Fans for internal rooms can switch on with the light or operate on a separate switch.

FINDING THE SPACE

Master suite ensemble If you aren't able to borrow space from an adjoining room, you will have to install your new amenities in an area of the bedroom. One possible arrangement is a false wall the length of the room, which may give space for storage as well.

For a small bedroom consider a shower cubicle, or a minute cabin-style bathroom that fits neatly into a corner. The basic kit consists of an enclosure with plumbingware and fixtures; the unit base converts to a tub.

The only solution in a really tiny room, if you are determined to have extra facilities, is a lavatory/shower unit with a fold-away tray that takes up very little space when not in use.

SPACE SAVERS

Look for ideas that will give you the maximum amenities in a small area.

Showers can be over the tub. A separate cubicle takes up less than a yard. Doors can open to the right or left. Space-saving doors slide, fold or pivot. Non-standard enclosures will fit below a sloping ceiling or in a dormer.

Tubs Compact or sit-up tubs available. Small corner bath may suit some layouts.

Lavatories Wall-hung lavatories free floor space; a vanity unit adds storage. A tiny bowl isn't ideal for general use.

A toilet that's wall-hung or close-coupled gives more floor space. Consider slim-line or built-in tanks. Waste can be pumped away through small-bore pipes if position of the soil stack is a problem. Check plumbing code for permissibility.

Bidets may be wall-hung or floor mounted.

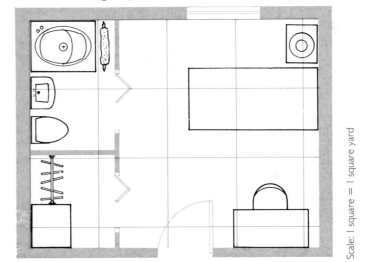

Scale: 1 square = 1 square yard

△ *Cupboard fitting*
Wooden louvered doors which blend easily with existing bedroom furnishings have been used here to convert a comparatively small area of a bedroom into a trim shower room. The space over the doors could be used for long-term storage.

▷ *Master suite storage*
In an alternative arrangement to the one shown above, a line of cupboards has been run along the entire length of the wall. This gives room for a walk-in clothes closet as well as a toilet and soak tub with shower above. A quiet flush toilet will allow a nearby sleeper to doze undisturbed. The plan shows the complete layout.

△ ▷ *Master suite*

If space isn't a problem, a luxury bed and bath suite that is as pleasing on the eye as it is pleasurable to use can be devised. Some manufacturers offer a broad range of matching furnishings for bed and bath areas – the room shown on the right has been designed as a natural extension of the bedroom. Even the bath paneling has a similar molding to that on the cupboard doors in the bedroom. Details such as gentle pastels and soft rugs in both rooms complete the scene of tranquil luxury. Opaque glazed doors ensure a degree of privacy but provide continuity as well.

If you're working to a smaller scale, adapt some of the ideas for a luxury finish. Woodwork can be matched in both areas, and consider using the same fabric at windows, behind glazed cupboards and to conceal the shower – you can hang waterproof shower curtains on the inside (see page 16).

*This modern master suite bathroom
shows how the two areas can share
decorative ideas to give a sense of
unity, although quite different
atmospheres can be created in keeping
with the separate functions. Lighting is
particularly important to set a mood:
here, the bedside lamp softly
illuminates the sleeping area. A wall-
hung lavatory can have plumbing
housed in a cabinet to provide storage
as well as giving a streamlined look.*

SEPARATE QUARTERS

An ideal solution to finding space for a
master suite bathroom would be to
adapt an adjacent small bedroom. This
may well allow you to go beyond the
basics: you could include a bidet in your
scheme, and a comfortable chair to relax in.

If you don't want to lose a bedroom,
a compromise would be to install the
new bathroom between two bedrooms, taking space from each but ensuring both rooms are still big enough to
function as bedrooms. Remember
always to get expert advice on plumbing and major structural alterations.

DOWN TO DETAILS

Plumbing comes in a wide range of
colors and styles. Dark-hued tubs and
lavatories aren't the easiest to keep
clean if the water is hard. If you want a
cast-iron tub, check that the floor is
sturdy enough to take the weight. Wall-
hung equipment, such as a toilet, should
be well supported on a stout wall.

Decoration of the new bathroom
should be linked to the bedroom
scheme to give a real master suite feel,
though the bathroom needn't have
identical treatment. If your bedroom
has muted, restful tones you could pick
out an accent color to give a livelier, refreshing note to the bathroom, perhaps
by introducing a little color and excite-
ment to accessories such as towels.

Wallcoverings will need to cope with
moisture: if the bathroom is tiny, complete tiling may be possible.

Flooring If you want to carry through
carpeting from the bedroom, protect
damp areas with a mat. Otherwise
choose tiles to blend with the bedroom
floor.

▷ *Arched elegance*
*An adjoining room is linked with an
arch to provide bath space. Cool
aquamarine tones are featured
throughout the vivid tiling surrounding
fixtures. Bathroom curtains and the
bed valance have been made in the
same fabric, with accessories picked
out in shaded tones.*

△ **Luxury shower**
This neo-angle shower stall unit provides a 10in.-deep shower receptor for luxurious foot bathing. An attractive seat, set in the back corner of the unit, allows the bather to dangle tired feet in a pool of water.

◁ **Tailored to suit**
Where space is tight it's worth seeking out storage designed to fit around plumbing. These units allow you to build up high with lean cupboards.

ELECTRICAL OUTLETS

Safety must come first in your plans. If you've taken space from a bedroom, have any electrical outlets removed as the only outlet you can have in a bathroom is a ground fault interrupter. Get expert advice on electrical installations.

Lighting must be altered if you're using a former bedroom. The switch should meet safety regulations and usually is installed outside the actual bathroom area. Have diffused general lighting with task lighting by the mirror for shaving and making-up.

Heating is important; there's nothing so dreary as a chilly bathroom. Look for special bathroom radiators or a heated towel rack. A wall-mounted heater should never be hung above a tub or within splashing range. Be cautious when using any electrical appliance in the bathroom.

◁ **Bold bathroom**
This bathroom has more dramatic treatment than the bedroom, but colors have been chosen to give a unifying effect. A folding door separates the areas without taking up much space.

You can leave toiletries on display in your master bathroom, which isn't usually desirable in a family bathroom.

THE FITNESS BATHROOM

Exercise your way to good health in the comfort of your home.

Until quite recently anyone doing regular workouts was dubbed a fitness fanatic or health freak. Not so today: we're all much more aware of the need to take care of our bodies. There's been a boom in health clubs that offer everything from pampering steam-rooms to punishing circuit training. But regular visits can be expensive and involve quite a commitment – and not everyone wants to pump iron in public!

An alternative is to install your own health center at home. The preliminary cost may be substantial: if you want anything but the simplest equipment, there's bound to be quite a lot of structural investigation, if not actual alteration, to be done. However, you'll have the benefit of exercising when you want with equipment that suits your needs.

Space for fitness If you're really avid and can find the space, you'll want the whole works – a mini gymnasium with workbench, wallbars, fitness machines, whirlpool bath, perhaps a sauna. On this scale you may need specialist advice, as you'll almost certainly have to adapt a spare room, take over a second bathroom or even abandon the bathroom completely and convert space at the back of the garage.

More modest schemes could include exercise equipment that folds away: some quite sophisticated systems stack flat against a wall. Take a long look at your bathroom and surrounding area. Would high-level storage release floor space? Maybe there's a landing area you can incorporate by moving a wall. If space is tight consider replacing a tub with a power shower, and fitness equipment that folds for easy storage.

Health combination
What better way to end a workout? This whirlpool bath combines the durable beauty of enameled cast iron with comfortable two-person bathing. A unique flush-mounted overflow permits bathers to recline at both ends of the tub.

◁ *Bubble bath*
Bath time is invigorating for children and adults alike with a whirlpool bath that gives adjustable degrees of turbulence. Air is pumped from small jets in the base of the bath, allowing you either to relax in gently massaging bubbles or submit yourself to energetic pummeling.

▽ *Steaming up*
After your workout, ease those tired muscles in the comfort of a steam enclosure. As well as a shower head, this one has retractable seating, recessed downlights — and you can even install moisture-proof speakers and relax to the gentle strains of music.

WATER TREATS

A whirlpool bath is pleasantly relaxing and may give temporary relief to arthritic or rheumatic joints, but take medical advice before using a whirlpool if you're pregnant or have a kidney problem. If you're unsure of what you want, some suppliers will let you try out different systems.

All whirlpool effects involve electric pumps so for safety's sake consider only specialist equipment and installation. Some pumps make quite a bit of noise so listen before you buy.

There are two main systems – the whirlpool jet (such as the Jacuzzi) re-circulates bath water mixed with air through outlets on the bath sides. The direction of the jet is adjustable. With the second system – air or spa baths – air is forced into the water through holes in the base and the backrest of the tub.

Whirlpools aren't cheap. If your tub is in good condition, a whirlpool effect can be added: portable units are available in the marketplace.

Health showers Adjustable showers with a multi-function shower head give a soft or torrent spray or invigorating needle jet. There are also massage shower heads or for all-over action body sprays may be used.

A steam shower may be ideal in a spare room or landing space. Any place that would be suitable for a shower stall unit is also appropriate for a steam shower. Shower stalls should be at least 3 feet wide for comfort.

Saunas A good-sized home sauna seats four or five; the cabin of a small sauna, seating two, is about 4ft. square. As well as bench and headrests, the cabin has a stove – usually electric nowadays, though wood burners are available – heat retaining rocks, a bucket and ladle, thermometer and light.

Assembly of a sauna kit isn't too difficult. No plumbing is required, but you need a power supply and an opened window or exhaust fan. Let a cold shower substitute for the traditional roll in the snow.

Before installing a sauna, have a medical checkup as intense heat can aggravate some conditions. Limit the time you spend in the sauna, initially.

◁ *Steam machine*
Steam treatment relaxes and refreshes a tired body. This attractive hexagonal cubicle has a seat so you can become steamed up at your leisure. A special unit generates steam at a preselected temperature for up to two hours.

△ *Heat treat*
A sauna is great for reviving a tired system, and it needn't take up too much space. This little cabin, custom-built to fit into an ordinary bathroom, uses the bath as a plunge pool so the really hardy can take a cold dip.

BRIGHT IDEA

An air bath mat placed in an existing tub gives a refreshing stream of bubbles. A pump produces a flow of air through tubing that leads to the mat, and plumbing or drilling into the tub aren't necessary. If you want an ordinary tub, simply remove the mat.

EQUIPPED FOR FITNESS

For a general program to increase well-being, aim for a balance of three main elements: aerobic exercise such as cycling, rowing or jogging; body toning – spot exercising one specific area, perhaps with weights; and relaxation/water treatment – a whirlpool bath, steam shower or sauna. Draw up a realistic timetable for your routine, and stick to it – the most elaborate and expensive gear won't get you in good shape if you don't use it.

To find exercise apparatus to suit your needs and the available space, shop around and try out as much as you can. Allow plenty of space in your initial calculations, and consider where apparatus will be stored so that it doesn't get in the way. Home fitness manufacturers are aware of space constraints in the average bathroom so there are plenty of fold-away and wall-mounted systems on the market.

The equipment available ranges from a complete workout system for serious exercise to a folding bike in a corner of the room. For the enthusiast without much space, a multi-trainer with bench and wallbars adapts for a variety of exercises and stacks against a wall after the workout.

If you shudder at the thought of anything rigorous, like an abdominal crunch press, why not spring into shape with one of the most fun ideas on the market – a mini-trampoline, or rebounder, on which you develop a nice rhythm while bouncing or skipping.

More conventional, and the most popular home exercise product, is an exercise bike: some convert into a rowing machine. Look for a bike with enclosed chain and smooth, quiet operation. On some the resistance can be increased for more strenuous exercise. Install a book clamp and catch up with some reading while you pedal.

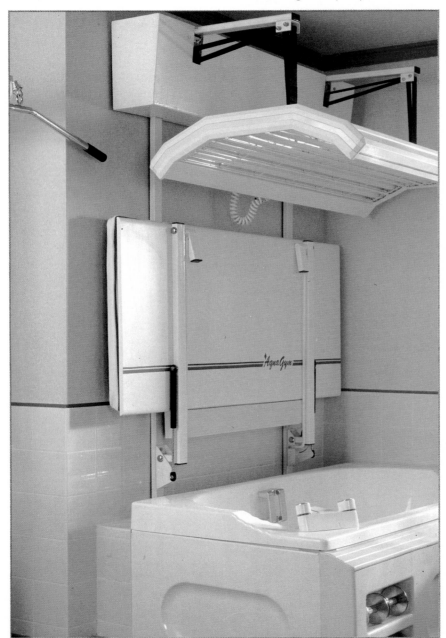

△ ◁ *Activity bathroom*
The facilities of a fitness center can be combined with the pleasures of a luxury bathroom: there's a whirlpool to refresh the spirit and ease tired muscles after exercising. A special storage panel on the tub holds weights or toiletries, and there's even a shelf for your waterproof, battery-operated personal stereo.

A space-saving idea (shown in the view on the left) is the massage/sun deck that folds flat against the wall to give access to the tub. The tanning canopy over the tub is raised and lowered at the touch of a button and stored near the ceiling. Always wear goggles, and follow manufacturer's instructions when using a tanning system.

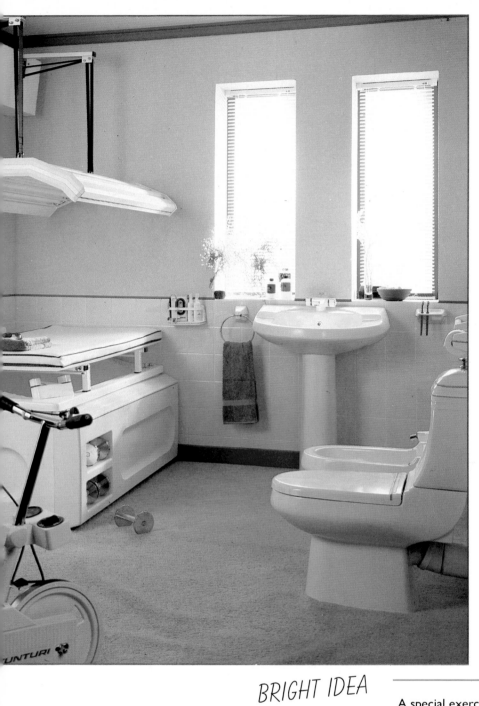

△ Wall workout

A wall-mounted home multi-exerciser with bench and wallbars can be used by several members of the family as it adapts for a variety of exercises to suit different levels of fitness. After use it all folds away to stack neatly against the wall.

When installing this sort of equipment make sure you attach it very securely to a wall – and floor – that's sturdy enough to take the strain.

BRIGHT IDEA

A special exercise mat is a sensible idea for a regular routine: apart from giving a soft base for your workout, a mat reduces noise and vibration and also protects floorcoverings from excessive wear. A carry strap holds the rolled mat neatly in place when it is not in use.

SAFELY FIT

Have a medical checkup before exercising if you're unfit or not in the best of health.

Don't start out by taking on an advanced routine; go gently at first.

Never exercise when you're too tired. If you feel any pain, stop immediately.

Exercise regularly, three or four times a week for twenty to thirty minutes, in a warm, well-ventilated room.

Wear comfortable clothing that doesn't restrict circulation, and breathe as normally as possible while you are doing your routine.

Do stretching exercises to warm up and cool down before and after your workout.

Use equipment according to manufacturer's instructions: make sure it's stored safely after use, particularly if there are small children around.

Allow plenty of room to use everything safely – don't underestimate how much space something like weights or a jump rope need.

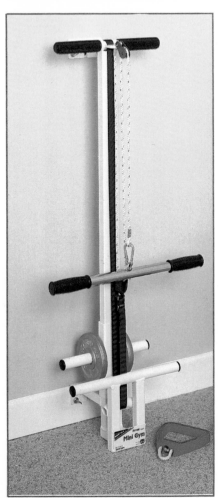

△ **Rowing power**
A rowing machine provides an in-house opportunity for cardiovascular exercise. It requires no installation and can be easily moved around the room or folded for storage.

▽ **Heavy metal**
A weight set consisting of ten weights has an attractive yet tough cover to keep you and your bathroom looking neat and trim. This set has a special screw attachment for quick weight changes.

◁ **Home health**
A mini-gym that quickly fits on wall studs or in a doorway can be used for up to thirty different exercises. It's quiet in operation, so would be ideal for an upstairs bathroom or apartment.

CREATIVE BATHROOM TILING

For the adventurous, imaginative use of tiling will add flair and originality to your bathroom.

Ceramic tiles have long been recognized as one of the most practical surfaces for a bathroom, particularly in areas likely to come into contact with water. For practical reasons, it's a sound idea to partially or fully tile a bathroom wall as well as tiling the casing and surrounds of fixtures such as tub and lavatory.

Much modern tile is of course pleasing to the eye as well as practical, and in recent years the options for creative use of tile have rapidly expanded. For the adventurous, this wide selection of tiles presents a challenge to put creativity to work designing a tile effect uniquely suited to individual bathroom requirements and personal taste.

There certainly is no shortage of possibilities with a splendid array of vibrant colors and unusual shapes, such as diamond, hexagonal and octagonal. The actual surface of a tile can be plain, raised, embossed, or incised. Patterns range from the prettily floral to modern geometric designs, with some also borrowing inspiration from a past era — there are many good copies of Victorian and Edwardian styles. Others, for example the high-tech metallic finishes, are distinctly modern. Mural tiles or richly decorated tile panels can create a focal point, and a broad range of attractive borders adds to the possibilities of creative tiling.

Before you let your imagination run wild, however, you must first sort out the practicalities. Start your initial planning by examining the shape and size of your room. Clever tiling can help to conceal flaws and highlight strengths. Which areas do you want to enhance, which would you prefer to fade into the background?

You must also study the surfaces. Are the walls square? Tiles produce such a perfect grid that flaws can be obvious. Use a carpenter's level to trace any fault, and plan so that a row of cut tiles falls in the least obvious place.

With such a wealth of ideas to choose from, remember mistakes can be costly. Spend some time planning the layout; it's too late to change your mind once the tiles are installed. When looking for inspiration, find pictures of finished rooms, rather than making decisions based on a small section of tiling: what can be pleasing in a small amount may prove to be overpowering on four walls.

Draw a plan of the walls and tiling positioning onto graph paper. Pin this up, with variations, in your bathroom and live with the idea for a while, until you are quite certain you have made the right choice.

If you are using standard-size tiles and your design is complex, invest in a grid that adheres to the wall, providing a framework for arranging the design so you can see the result before you cement your tiles in place. Alternatively, lay the tiles down on a large flat surface to check the positioning.

Plain and patterned
A combination of different small, chunky tiles has been grouped to provide an attractive patchwork effect around a wash area. Note how they have been symmetrically arranged to give an unobtrusive sense of order to the overall design.

△ **Seaside theme**
The white tiling in this bathroom is enhanced with coral and green images of sea life. A picturesque combination of tiles frames the mirror and window. Shell accessories enhance the marine theme.

◁ **Tiling partners**
Two complementary methods of finishing off a panel of plain tiles: a pretty floral border echoes wall and curtain pattern, while a top layer provides a neat zigzag finish. If you want to create a similar effect, take care when cutting diagonals to ensure they are the same size as the square tiles, as a diagonal cut through the center will obviously be longer than the outside edge.

MAINLY PLAIN

Very handsome effects can be produced by imaginative use of plain tiles, either on their own or combined with more decorative styles. Ordinary whites and neutrals are generally less expensive than vivid hues, but if you are tempted by anything particularly vibrant make sure you won't tire of the result after a while.

Tiles can be prohibitively expensive. If you want to keep costs down, consider budget-priced plain tiles for most of the area with the addition of more extravagant special effects such as borders or decorative inserts of single tiles, panels or even a tiled mural. Remember, though, if you use tiles from different sources make sure they are of equal thickness.

With clever positioning, plain tiles on their own are subtly pleasing. Square and rectangular tiles can be laid stepped, in bricklaying fashion, while square tiles laid diagonally look handsome – they often create a more spacious effect than those laid in the conventional, straight method.

For good looks at low cost, consider using colored grouting with budget-priced plain tiles, which gives a very effective fine grid of color. Grouting can be bought in a variety of colors.

△ *Blue mood*
Overall tiling in deep colors can produce dramatic impact, but to avoid too dense a result introduce variations on your theme. Here, different tones of vibrant blue tiles are laid diagonally on walls but conventionally straight on other surfaces to add interest.

◁ *Tiled panels*
As an alternative to the overall scheme of rich blue tiles pictured above, a more neutral background can be used to give a lighter result, with the addition of distinctive panels and borders. The panels, large or small, can be designed to suit the size and shape of your room.

BORDER STORY

One of the most attractive ideas to give a fine finish to tiling is through introducing a border. These can vary from delicate bands of fine pattern to bold, wide friezes. Borders can be added at ceiling or dado level, or can round off a partly tiled surface.

Running a border or frieze around the room at dado height can help draw together aspects of an awkwardly shaped room, and may give an impression of more pleasing proportions. A border can also frame attractive features – a pretty mirror, perhaps, or a window.

Tiles specifically designed as borders are frequently manufactured to complement a broad range of tile. They are often narrow rectangles, flat or raised. Modern versions of Victorian dado tiles are available, with the tiles ending in a raised "bullnose."

You could experiment by creating your own borders. Colored or patterned tiles can border contrasting styles, or you can build up a checkerboard effect with colored tiles. The cumulative effect of a broad band of several rows can be dramatic, or consider swooping diagonal patterns across a large field of tiles on one or more walls. These more original creative ideas can give a great deal of satisfaction, but they do need conviction and careful thinking through at the planning stage before you commit yourself to any expenditure.

△ *Sunny spots*
Splashes of yellow on tile and accessories relieve the starkness of pristine white. Note how disparate elements can be drawn together through careful use of accent color.

▷ *Simply classic*
A subtle variation in tile positioning: large off-white wall tiles are stepped in brick fashion rather than laid conventionally in straight vertical rows. A black and white checkered border adds interest at dado level, and white floor tiles bordered by black complete the sophisticated effect.

◁ **Tiling trim**

As well as breaking up plain runs of tile, contrasting colors or patterns can be used to draw the eye towards focal points in the bathroom. Here, a mock dado in white and pink is extended to border the mirror, creating a pretty feature.

▽ **Plain and pattern**

There is a wide variety of different plain and patterned tiles on the market that can be arranged to suit your individual specifications. In this alternative arrangement of the lavatory area pictured left, the tile section under the mock dado has a trellis pattern. The floral-edged border is also used to frame a mirror.

▽ **Dashing dado**

To relieve a large, bland stretch of tile, decorative tiles can be added to provide interest at dado height. This border undulates around the room adding a cheerful demeanor to an otherwise muted color scheme.

BRIGHT IDEA

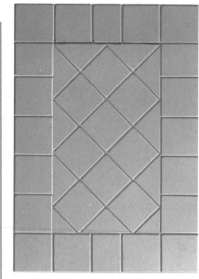

Diagonal tile installation can add a subtle dimension to plain tiles. Blocks of diagonals bordered by rows of straight tiling can create stylish geometric patterns.

Tiles laid on the diagonal take up more space than those laid straight, so work out the positioning of adjacent diagonal and straight tiles carefully. Plot the whole panel on graph paper before you start. If necessary, trim the center tile, as shown above, for a neat finish.

△ *Framing with tile*
Clever positioning of plain tiles can produce a very distinguished result. Here, a window with a blind is made into a decorative feature by skillful use of a soft green tiled surround – the tiles are built up above the window to form a handsome centerpiece within the framework provided by the gently contrasting wall.

Elsewhere in the same room the effect of long stretches of floor-to-ceiling tiling on facing walls is partly relieved by an ornate bamboo frame and decorative fan.

△ *Proud border*
Attractive raised borders can be used to create a dado on a plain run of tiles, or to highlight points of interest in a bathroom. This border is available in a wide range of subtle colors.

▷ *Accessory details*
A novel way of introducing pattern to plain tiled walls: these stylish tile details make a decorative feature of bathroom accessories such as towel hooks and soap dishes.

INSTALLING A TUB SURROUND

You can give your bathroom a new look by changing the paneling down the side of the bath — or create a luxurious and dramatic effect with a new surround.

Modern tubs come complete with molded panels that clip into place to hide the underside of the tub, and the supply and drain pipes. They are convenient and easy to install, but may not fit in with your decor. In older homes, there may be problems. Flimsy hardboard panels around the sides of the tub may have deteriorated, or perhaps you want to change an existing panel.

You can buy matching shaped plastic or fiberglass aprons for many modern tubs these days. And there are even curved panels to cope with corner tubs. However, if you want to decorate the sides of your tub enclosure in some other way, you can achieve surprisingly dramatic effects by enclosing the side yourself.

The principle is the same, whatever material you choose to use for the cladding and decoration. You start by building a simple framework of soft-wood posts and rails along the sides and end of the tub, and then attach the cladding material to this.

CHOOSING A FINISH

The cladding material can either be a finish in itself, or a surface to which you can add your chosen finish. For example, a designed mahogany panel or an old pine door can be installed around the sides of a tub for a traditional look. For a more rustic effect, tongue-and-groove boards, either varnished or painted, are a suitable choice. If your bathroom has a carpeted floor, you can even run the carpet up the side of the tub, though a better choice might be sheet vinyl to match existing flooring, or ceramic tiles to match the tub surround.

You could use hardboard if you plan to paper the panels, but the best bet (if you want to tile the panels) is plywood. Don't use chipboard in a bathroom because it swells and warps out of shape if it gets wet.

For the same reason, any hardboard you use should be the oil-tempered variety, and plywood should be at least exterior grade.

ALLOWING FOR ACCESS

A vital point to bear in mind when enclosing anything, is that you might need access to it at some time in the future. For example, you may need to get at the waste trap of a tub if you have a blockage. If you think about this point at the planning stage, it's generally a simple matter either to make the paneling easy to remove, or to incorporate some sort of access hatch.

Tiled panel
This bath has been enclosed with a plywood panel that has then been tiled over. Similar panels are built in at the end and side of the room.

PLANNING THE JOB

Once you have decided that you want to enclose your tub and what type of finish you want on the apron, you have to start planning the job in a little more detail. It is simplest to fit an apron flush with the side of the tub, but if you have the space and have some experience of woodwork, it is attractive to build a shelf at the same time as the paneling, so that the panel is about 6in. out from the side of the tub. You need to measure the tub so you can sketch out the framework and work out how much wood you'll need for it, what size cladding panels will be required, and how you will make the various joints.

RABBET JOINTS

To make up the framework supporting the tub surround described in this chapter you have to make a fairly simple joint, called a rabbet joint. It is used when you want to make a T-shaped join between two pieces of wood.

| Measure and mark the joint ▷
In this example, the rebate to be cut is 1in. × 1in., set into a 2in. square batten (furring strip). Using a try square, mark around three sides of the batten, 1in. from the top. Mark across the top and down the sides, 1in. from the front.

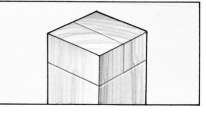

2 Make the first cut ▷
Set the batten upright in a workbench and use a backsaw to saw down from the top, following the marked line, until you reach the line marked around the batten. It is very important that both the pencil marks and the saw cut are accurate, to get a good fit and a perfect right angle.

3 Make the second cut
Turn the batten on its side, so it protrudes from the end of the workbench and cut downwards, following the line marked across the batten, until you meet the previous cut and the waste block of wood comes out.

4 Screwing the joint together ▷ ▷
Look at the batten to be set into the joint you have made, and check the fit. Chisel or saw away any surfaces that protrude. Mark screw positions so they are staggered (to avoid splitting the wood). Remove the batten and drill clearance holes through the batten, plus countersunk holes for the heads of the screws. Check the batten again, and use an awl to mark the other half of the joints. Use a fine drill to make pilot holes a few fractions into the cut half of the joint. Apply woodworking adhesive to all parts of the joint that meet. Position the batten and screw firmly in place.

TOENAILING

This is a useful technique for making a T-shaped joint between fairly substantial battens (in this case 1in. × 2in. and 2in. square). It is a quick and easy jointing method, but should only be used where the joint is to be covered (inside a stud wall, or behind a tub surround, for example). Also, it is only suitable if the other end of the upright part of the T is to be firmly located. In the situation where toenailing is used here (under the tub) the cross bar of the T-joint is attached firmly to the floor first.

| Position the upright ▷
Set the upright on the cross bar and use a pencil to mark its position (so you can ensure it is still in the right place when the nailing is finished). Temporarily nail a piece of discarded wood so that one edge of it butts up to the upright. (Clamp it in place rather than nailing, if this is possible.)
Using a 3in. oval wire nail, drive it in at an angle through the upright, into the cross piece, positioning it about a third of the way across the width of the battens – in this case, about ⅝in. in from the front edges of the two battens to be joined. (Oval nails are used to prevent the wood from splitting.)

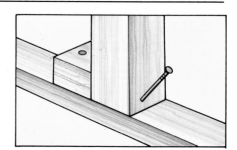

2 Nail in the other direction
Remove the piece of waste wood, and renail it on the other side of the joint. Drive in a second nail from the other side, positioning it two-thirds of the way across the joint (i.e. the nails are evenly spaced across the joint).

INSTALLING A TUB SURROUND

The framework can be made of rough lumber. As with all carpentry work, it is important to plan the work carefully before you start and make accurate measurements at each stage. These instructions are for fitting a side *and* end panel, with adjustments for fitting a side panel where appropriate.

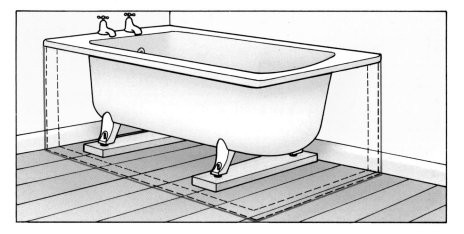

1 Measure around the tub
Start by measuring the length of each panel, and decide on the locations of the supports. Check that there will be no problems installing in place (poor plasterwork, missing floorboards, etc.) and prepare as necessary. You will probably need a batten attached to the wall at each end of the area to be paneled, two battens along the side and one at the corner (if necessary).

2 Cut wood for bottom rails △
Determine the exact length of each of the bottom rails: subtract the thickness of the paneling, plus any decorative finish, from each measurement, and subtract 2in. from the width of the tub to give the measurement of the end rail (to allow for the dimension of the side rail).
(There is no need to subtract anything from the measurement of the length of the tub if you are attaching a side panel only.) Cut two pieces of 2in. × 1in. wood for bottom rails.

3 Install bottom rails ▷
Lay the rails on the floor directly beneath (and parallel to) the lip of the tub, checking their alignment with a carpenter's level if necessary. Mark their positions with pencil lines. Now set them back from the marked lines by the thickness of cladding material plus any decorative finish (e.g., tiles), to allow the panel to finish neatly below the tub lip. Nail the battens to a wood floor (beware of pipes running too close to the surface), or plug and screw them in place if the tub is on a solid floor.

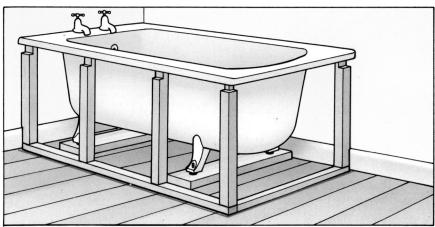

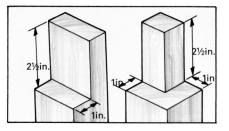

4 Measure and cut uprights △
Then measure the distance between the underside of the tub beneath the lip, and the top edge of the floor battens. Cut pieces of 2in. square wood to this length plus 1/16in. for the uprights; you'll need four to panel in a tub side, or five if you are paneling an end as well. Following the instructions opposite, use your backsaw to cut out a 2½in. × 1in. rabbet joint at one end of each post, ready to accept the 2in. × 1in. top rail later (the extra ¼in. is to allow for any overhang of the tub lip). Cut the rabbet both ways on the corner post if you are also doing the end of the tub.

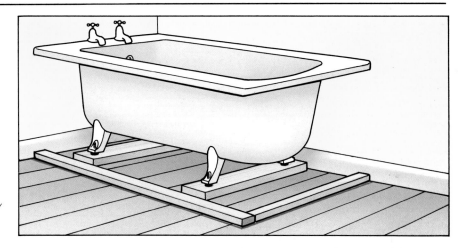

5 Install the uprights △
Wedge the posts into place between the floor battens and the tub lip, with the rabbets at the top, facing out into the room. For two panels, position one post against each wall at the ends of the long and short panels, one at the corner and two more equally spaced down the long side of the tub. (For a single panel you should position one upright against the wall at each end, with the other two equally spaced between.) Scribe the end posts to fit around the baseboard if necessary. The extra 1/16in. in length should ensure that they are a tight fit. Check that they are vertical in each direction using your carpenter's level. Then toenail their feet to the floor battens, and screw the two end battens to the walls.

6 *Install top rails*
Measure and cut to length the 2in. × 1in. top rail(s) to match the bottom rail(s). Hold them up to the rabbets you cut in the tops of the battens, drill clearance and countersinking holes, and glue and screw them to the tops of the posts. If you try to nail them, you risk knocking the battens out of alignment.

7 *Install cladding panels ▷*
Measure for each panel and cut it to size. If you are fitting two panels, remember to add the thickness of the panel to the lengthwise measurement to get a neat finish at the corner. You may need to divide the side panel into two sections to get access to the waste trap: this will depend on the choice of the paneling material. A single mahogany panel, for example, can be fitted with six screws, so that the whole panel is removed for access. On the other hand, if the panel is to be tiled, you only want a small access panel, so split the side panel into two parts, one to fit the 'bay' between the first two posts at the faucet end of the bath, the other to fit the rest of the tub side. Then hold up each panel to the

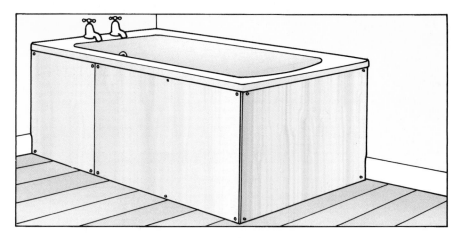

framework and scribe the ends to fit around base moldings if necessary. Drill pilot and countersinking holes along each edge of the larger panel at around 15-20in. intervals and screw the panel to the framework. Fix the smaller panel with mirror screws drilling pilot holes first. Do not fit the decorative heads on mirror screws at this point, and do not tighten them if you are planning to tile the panels.

8 *Apply finish*
If the paneling is to be decorated, seal it with a coat of sizing ready for papering (a vinyl wallcovering is best in a bathroom), or with a coat of diluted PVA adhesive if you plan to tile it. Paper over the screws, then replace their decorative heads. If you are tiling the removable access panel, remove each corner screw and drill through the tile that will cover it at the appropriate point with a masonry drill. Install the tile in position, drive screws back in and fit the decorative heads.

FITTING A PANEL AND SURROUND

◁ *Building the framework*
The framework for a tub apron with platform has to be slightly more substantial than for a straight panel. Use 2in. square wood with rabbet joints as indicated. Measure and cut all the joints first. All the uprights are the same length as the finished height of the box, less the thickness of the paneling (see inset, top right). Rabbet joints are cut at each end of the uprights, facing inwards to make installation easier. Cut rabbet recesses in the horizontal elements of the framework to accept the uprights and the cross members at the top used to support the paneling. At the corner, the two inner horizontal struts interlock to make a firm joint (see inset, bottom right).

▷ *Bathroom luxury*
If you can spare the room, a 'peninsular' bath with a wide platform creates a really luxurious effect. In a less spacious room, you can still add the platform on two sides to provide a shelf for ornaments and toiletries, without having to move the bath itself. Note how a paneled effect has been created by applying extra wooden strips around the edge of the panels, tacking and gluing it in place. Moldings fitted inside the recess create a traditional flavor. The panels must be thoroughly sanded and primed before applying under- and topcoats of paint.

SHOWER STALL ROOMS

When space is tight, building a shower room may be the logical alternative to a conventional bathroom.

Showers are more economical than baths – they're quick and easy, they use less hot water and they take up less space. A shower stall room is also easier and less expensive to install than a bathroom, and children love showers.

The shower These days choosing a shower valve and a shower head can be as perplexing as choosing an appliance. Different shower valves and heads perform different features. It is a good idea to visit a showroom where you can compare both performance and style.

Some special options available today are quite practical. One such feature prevents scalding by a control that maintains water temperatures even when the water is being used elsewhere in the house.

Shower heads are available in different styles and colors to match the bathroom in which they are being installed. Many manufacturers now offer a water-saving feature along with the optional massage sprays and flexible tubing for hand-held or stationary use.

Less common options include an adjustable wall bar for height adjustment and multiple showerheads for body spraying.

Because you can adjust them to the height of the user, hand-held showerheads are more flexible than, but not as neat as stationary ones. With pressure-balancing controls, hot and cold water pressures are read and fluctuating water pressure is adjusted. A thermostatically controlled valve is able to read the actual temperature and adjust accordingly.

Shower stalls need to be fully waterproof. They must be enclosed on two or three sides, with a door or shower curtain on the remaining side(s).

Stylish simplicity

Shower stalls open up exciting decorating possibilities for a small bathroom. They are available in many shapes, sizes and colors. Here, a neo-angle unit fits neatly into the corner. The clear glass panels, trimmed with black door frames, add to the contemporary style of this room.

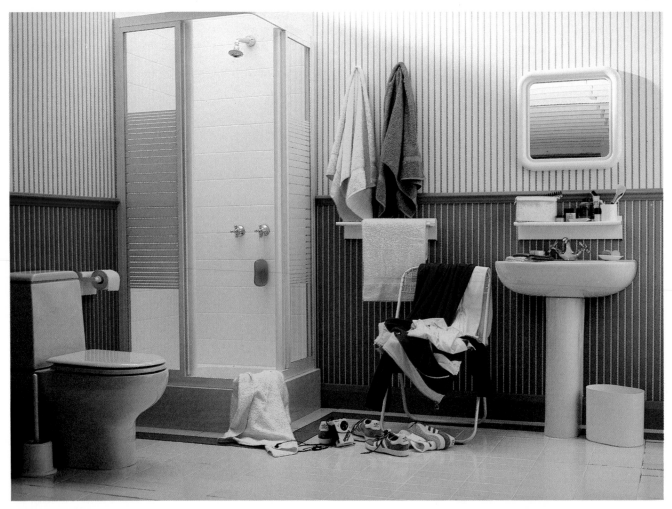

Shower enclosures come ready-built, but for more versatility, there is a wide selection of kit showers. Made of fiberglass or plastic, these comprise of back and side panels with a choice of corner opening, bi-fold, sliding and curved corner door options. If you want to fit a shower into an oddly shaped space, it is worth considering tiling the entire area, including the floor (using non-slip tiles), and using a shower door or curtain over the entrance.

Shower bases are usually made from ceramic, enameled steel or acrylic and come in a range of sizes, the most common being 30in., 32in. and 36in. square, although there are also rectangular and corner models.

Practicalities You need to consider plumbing, safety and ventilation. So ask your local authority about the regulations governing the installation of showers and drainage connections before starting any work.

It is usually fairly straightforward to run water to the shower but connecting the drainage can be more difficult. The length and pitch of the waste pipe is not as critical as with a toilet but placing the shower stall against an outside wall and near to other plumbing units makes things easier.

Flooring In a shower room, the flooring should be water resistant as well as

△ *Green and yellow*
Coordinating vinyl wallcoverings are used above and below the bright green dado rail in this cheerful shower stall room. Vinyl is ideal in a bath or shower stall room – it has a thick coating that is water resistant.

The flooring has been chosen for its practicality and good looks. The white tiles are bordered with green for definition. Ceramic tiles get slippery when wet so it's wise to add a floor rug with a rubber, non-slip backing or underlay.

good looking. There are plenty of choices. Vinyl tiles or cushion flooring is comfortable to stand on and is easily cleaned, and there are hundreds of styles and patterns to choose from. Wood flooring sealed with polyurethane varnish is warm and practical and harmonizes with most color schemes. Ceramic tiles are a traditional bathroom or shower flooring; they are beautiful and very hardwearing but more expensive and feel cold and hard.

If, however, you prefer the warmth of carpet, it is best to go for the ridged, rubber-backed kind made specifically for use in bathrooms. Ordinary carpet eventually rots if it is continually splashed with water.

BRIGHT IDEA

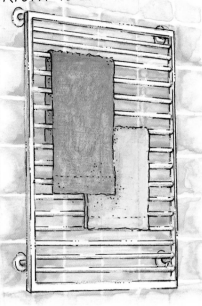

Towel warmer A single heated towel rack is rarely sufficient to heat a bathroom or shower stall room, while a conventional radiator doesn't give much towel hanging space. An alternative is to fit a stylish towel warmer with horizontal bars, available in a variety of heights.

DECORATION

A shower stall room has to be practical but there's no reason why it can't look good too – you can use as much imagination here as in any other room in the house. But because it's got to survive splashes of water, wet feet and even the occasional flood, surfaces need to be waterproof and easily dried.

The area inside the shower itself must be totally waterproof. It can be tiled or paneled but make sure that waterproof adhesive and grouting is used for the tiles and any gaps into which water might seep are properly sealed with a flexible sealant.

Outside the shower area, bear in mind, that as well as splashes of water, condensation can be a problem. Wall tiles are ideal but paint, preferably an oil-based one, is an inexpensive alternative as long as the walls are smooth. Gloss is scrubbable and stands up well to moisture. If you prefer wallcovering, choose a vinyl or water-resistant finish.

This large powder room has enough space for a shower enclosure as well as a lavatory and toilet. The corner

shower stall is a good choice, ensuring a protected space for the toilet and there is plenty of room for hanging clothes and towels.

Here, it is decorated in three very different ways. The basic room remains the same – the walls inside the shower are tiled in white and the plain white fixtures are the perfect foil for a variety of color schemes from gentle peach to starker pink and black.

Scale: 1 square = 1 square yard

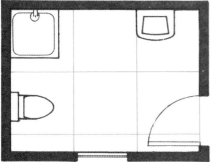

▽ Soft and practical

A striped waterproof wallcovering in a soft yellow, peach and gray with a coordinating border is teamed with a silver gray paint job.

The area below the dado rail is gloss painted in pale yellow; this is an inexpensive and attractive alternative to tiles. Flooring is honey-colored vinyl, sealed to protect it from water staining or seeping through the joints.

◁ Paint effect

Here, the walls are rag rolled in shades of pink for a softer, sophisticated effect, and then protected with several layers of clear matte polyurethane varnish, which creates a hard-wearing surface.

The floor is covered with black and white vinyl tiles arranged in a checkered pattern, while the horizontal line detail from the shower stall is picked up on the towel warmer (see Bright Idea).

INSTALLING A SHOWER

If space is at a premium, it may be worth considering abandoning the idea of a bathtub completely in favor of a shower room in a small house or apartment. It is also a compact solution if you want a second bathroom.

A self-contained enclosure takes up barely one square yard of floor space. As well as in the bathroom itself, there are plenty of other places where a shower can be installed: the corner of a bedroom, possibly behind cabinet doors; in an unused alcove; at the end of a corridor; even under the stairs.

It's no good installing a shower into such a tight corner that there's no room outside the cubicle to keep towels or to undress or dry yourself, so allow a minimum of 30in. square.

Space Look at the sizes of shower trays and enclosures carefully before buying. It may be tempting to fit a very small one into a tiny area but make sure it is big enough to use comfortably. Don't be afraid to climb inside the enclosure in the showroom to see how it feels.

SAFETY

Water and electricity make dangerous partners but, used properly, can be perfectly safe.

If fixtures are likely to get wet, make sure you choose those that are enclosed. Pull-cord switches are a safe type to use in a bathroom.

The only outlets you should ever have in a bathroom or shower stall room are ground fault interrupter outlets, which have such a low cut-out point that the chance of getting a shock is virtually nil.

Large electrical appliances, such as wall heaters or washing machines must be permanently wired into a sealed outlet and positioned out of reach of anyone using water.

◁ *Custom angles*
By introducing an angled custom shower arrangement, this shower stall room was dramatically improved. An angled lavatory and toilet were used as well. These shapes most efficiently used the small wall space, while maintaining an adequate walkway for the bathroom user.

Handmade Italian ceramic tiles in white and sea-foam green, with a rope border trim, create a cool, pleasing atmosphere. Classically styled cabinetry and moldings complete the overall space.

◁ **Many choices**
Not only are shower stalls available in many colors and sizes, they also come framed or frameless. The open design shown here is an extremely contemporary look. As well as providing friction-free door movement, the colored header and virtually invisible doors make a simple elegant statement in any environment.

▽ **Small space solution**
One end of a narrow bedroom has been turned into a tiny shower area. There is just enough space to stand between the vanity and the shower pan.

A simple waterproof curtain hangs across the entrance and the walls are covered with textured vinyl.

Hollywood-style cosmetic strip lights add a touch of glamor – make sure if buying lighting like this, that it's suitable for bathrooms.

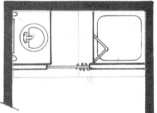

Scale: I square = I square yard

SHOWER ROOM STYLE

As shower stall rooms are usually far from large, color schemes are best kept simple to help create a feeling of space.

However, decorating a small room does give you the opportunity to be more adventurous or to use more expensive materials than in the main rooms of the house.

◁ *Curtain effect*
Extravagant layers of pleated and frilled curtains turn a simple white shower into something special.

This is not quite as impractical as it at first seems. The draperies are made from an easy-care synthetic fabric and underneath is a waterproof shower curtain.

△ *Economical choice*
Hiding the plumbing behind a false wall keeps this small space neat. The shower area is completely tiled and the rest of the room is papered with a washable vinyl that picks up the grid pattern of the tiles. A standard lavatory would not leave enough room here, so a narrow space-saving one is used.

▷ *Rug scheme*
The color scheme for this shower stall room with a corner cubicle is inspired by the Oriental dhurrie rug. The colors used as accents in the rug become the main elements – white floor and fixtures and blue tiled walls.

The division between floors and walls is sharply defined by two rows of rust tiles – the strongest color in the rug.

If you decide to have a floor rug in the shower or bathroom, it is wise to use a non-slip rubber padding, available at carpet shops or department stores, to avoid accidents.

POWDER ROOMS

A separate bathroom is a useful addition to most homes – making provision for one can be easier than you think.

For anyone sharing a home with young children, teenagers or elderly people, or regular overnight guests, the advantages of an additional bathroom, particularly one at the main level, are self-evident. It relieves congestion during family rush hours and saves children and adults the problem of having to climb flights of stairs in a large house and it also means guests don't ever have to use the main bathroom.

More often than not, installing a separate powder room is both feasible and economical; it can even improve the value of your home. But draw up your plans in consultation with an architect or plumber familiar with local building and plumbing codes. The installation of a new toilet, or any plumbing work that modifies or adds to the existing waste system, must be approved by your local building inspector.

Planning considerations A separate toilet can be fitted into a surprisingly small space. The optimum dimensions of approximately 42in. by 36in. allow room for a standard toilet with a 20in.-wide tank and 27in. projection together with a compact wall-mounted lavatory.

Any plans to install a toilet depend on the location of the existing soil stack to which it is to be connected by a waste pipe, 4in. in diameter. An ideal location would be below (or above) an existing bathroom, as it is possible to create additional access to the soil stack at ground floor level, although this is definitely a job for a professional.

The distance from the toilet base to the soil stack should be as short as possible for its gravity-fed drainage system to work efficiently. Sometimes it can be extended by a branch if you decide to put the second toilet in a room next to the existing bathroom.

The new small bore units, which are connected directly behind the pan, enable a toilet to be installed almost anywhere in the building, including a basement or attic. Compact and unobtrusive, they incorporate an efficient macerator that finely breaks up waste on flushing; an electrically powered pump discharges it through $7/8$in. pipework horizontally to a soil stack up to 65ft. away. But remember that this system requires you to have special approval from your local authority before proceeding.

Ventilation A window that opens is not obligatory. But in the absence of one, the building code demands that ample ventilation be provided by an exhaust fan (mounted in the ceiling or an external wall). The exhaust fan can come on automatically together with the light, or be operated by a separate switch or a simple timer mechanism.

Neat and narrow
A separate powder room is often confined to a long, narrow space making careful planning and decoration essential.

MAKING THE MOST OF SPACE

As most toilets are small, it's best to choose fixtures that use space as economically as possible.

The toilet While most toilet bases conform to a standard size, tanks are made in different dimensions. The smallest, generally made of plastic with a front flushing action, is as little as 4½in. deep. For a neater toilet, you might opt for the type where the entire tank is concealed behind a partition about 6in. deep. Wall-hung toilets are another good idea, making a restricted floor area easier to clean.

The lavatory In a narrow room, a small powder room basin is perfectly adequate – some project no more than 6in. into the room with part of the bowl recessed into the wall. In a more generous space, a vanity lavatory inset into a countertop or small storage cabinet is more useful.

Storage Although not essential, making some provision for storage could provide a helpful addition from overflow rooms elsewhere in the home. In a standard powder room with the toilet at one end, the wall space around the toilet might provide a good spot for a variety of shelves and cupboards.

If you have a downstairs powder room, it may be worthwhile to make provisions for hanging coats and hats – either hooks on the wall or door, or a traditional stand with a slot to hold umbrellas. In this way, the bathroom will perform dual roles. A full-length mirror, perhaps on the back of the door, is a useful addition and creates the illusion of space.

▷ *Elegant solution*

Even a tiny powder room, such as this one, can have elegance and style. The dado rail is covered with a high relief wallcovering and two large mirrors set parallel help to create space. A shiny silver sink and fabric-covered ceiling add touches of luxury.

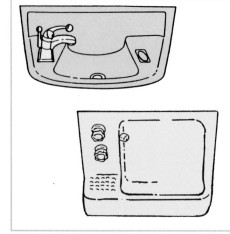

SPACE-SAVING LAVATORIES

All these wall-mounted lavatories leave the floor area free from plumbing. Those on the left are set into the wall, which must be able to take the recessed part of the unit. The shapes on the right are slightly deeper but are simpler to install. They include a corner sink and one with faucet neatly positioned on one side.

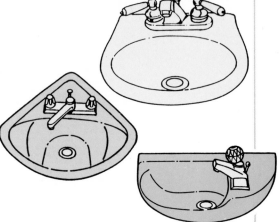

▷ Boxed-in

Pipes that run through this room from floor to ceiling to the right of the toilet are hidden behind pine paneling, which also includes a set of open shelves. The paneling has been extended to cover the entire back wall and floor.

A turquoise roman blind, towels and accessories liven up the honey-colored woodwork.

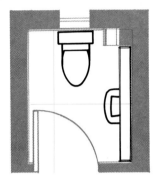

Scale: 1 square = 1 square yard

▽ Pretty pink

A wall-hung toilet and lavatory may involve additional installation work, but they do leave the floor completely free from obstructions. Such streamlined fixtures create clean lines in a small room.

▽ ▷ Making space

Another way to maximize the amount of free floor space is to install a toilet with a narrow tank, which keeps the entire fixture closer to the wall. To enlarge the room further, a wall-size mirror topped by recessed downlights is installed.

CHOOSING A SUITABLE PLACE

In addition to proximity to the soil stack, where you choose to install a powder room is limited by the requirement that a room containing a toilet must not open directly into a living room or kitchen, if possible and, for obvious reasons, a ventilated lobby in between is desirable.

As a hallway can act as a ventilated area (providing the doors to the adjoining rooms are left in place), a toilet can be created in the space below the stairs. But first consider its size: while it may conform in length and width to the minimum already mentioned, is it high enough? If the door is to open outwards into the hall, will it clash with other doors close by?

Good ventilation is also necessary. If there is no external wall, you can install a ceiling-mounted exhaust fan, provided it can extract into an attic above or ducts can connect it to the outside.

A toilet can be placed along a wall, in an alcove or in a separate section of the bathroom. Most toilets are 20-24in. wide and protrude 27-30in. out from the wall.

If space is a concern, a one-piece toilet is the better choice. They are only 19 or 20in. high while two-piece toilets are 26-28in. high.

A utility room If a utility room adjoins the kitchen, it is sometimes possible to borrow a small space to create a down-stairs powder room. Depending on its size and the appliances housed within it, some judicious doubling up could free the required extra space. Try stacking the dryer on top of the washing machine or investing in a combined washer/drier; sacrificing a chest freezer for a more space-saving upright one; or replacing a large sink with a smaller model, smart enough to act as a lavatory.

Position the toilet at the far end of the room, separated by a partition wall and door, and the reduced-size utility room now acts as the ventilated space.

△ *Dual purpose*
This powder room serves two roles. As well as taking pressure off the main bathroom, it provides the avid gardener with a home for geraniums during winter frosts. The cupboard below the inset lavatory keeps gardening equipment out of sight.

BRIGHT IDEA

A practical innovation This new type of macerator toilet can solve the problem of installing a toilet in a place where a connection with the soil stack cannot be made either easily or cheaply. The version that is shown here allows dirty water flowing from a small hand lavatory to be discharged at the same time as the waste from the toilet itself.

Upstairs Installing an additional powder room off a bedroom or on a landing is practical when space permits. If you are planning a bath or shower stall room to service the main bedroom, take into account the location of the existing plumbing. It may be more realistic to switch rooms if another, nearby bedroom allows for easier conversion.

Unlike the previous examples, there are no regulations to prevent you from having a toilet leading directly from a bedroom, but some form of soundproofing is important. The quieter though more expensive, syphon flush toilet is a good choice, and wood panel-ing, carpet and acoustic ceiling tiles help to reduce noise levels, both human and mechanical!

While many older homes have an upstairs toilet separate from the bathroom, most newer houses do not. It is, however, often possible to construct a partition wall to separate the toilet. If the layout of the bathroom makes it difficult to provide the separate toilet with its own entrance door, consider extending the partition wall only partway along the room. This, at least, provides some privacy if members of the family need to use the bathroom at the same time.

▽ *Dramatic decor*
Colorful peacocks adorn the walls and ceiling of this powder room, making it into something extraordinary. Birds carved into a delicate wood mirror frame repeat the wild bird theme. A faux-marble vanity and designer sink equipped with brass-and-porcelain fixtures are color coordinated.

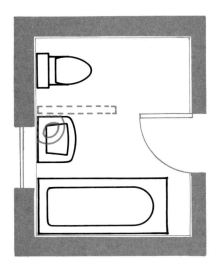

△ **Dividing the bathroom**
If you want to separate the toilet from the tub and lavatory, building a partition wall is not difficult. If, as in the plan shown above, creating a separate opening for the toilet would be complicated, consider ending the partition wall part of the way along the length of the room, creating some privacy if not a separate room. A corner sink against the partition helps to make the bathroom area roomier.

Scale: 1 square = 1 square yard

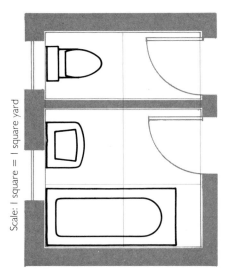

▽ **Old fashioned**
This replica of an old-fashioned toilet with an overhead-style tank is as efficient as the modern models and adds to the vintage feeling in this powder room at the same time. A neutral color scheme adds to the country style.

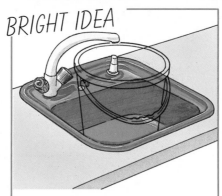

BRIGHT IDEA

A practical sink It's often handy to be able to use a kitchen-style lavatory to wash delicate clothing or to fill buckets of water for cleaning floors and washing the car. If there is room, install a deep kitchen sink with a tall faucet rather than a small lavatory – modern sinks are made in many attractive colors.

△ **Traditional style**
This classically simple room has been furnished with an elegant combination of mahogany woodwork, gleaming faucets and a matching blue-and-white inset china lavatory and towel holder.

The toilet tank is built into the back wall of the room, leaving only an unobtrusive flush button visible. When building in a tank, it is wise to make provision for repairs to be effective.

A SIMPLE BATHROOM WITH STYLE

This bathroom is as stylish as it is functional. Neutral backgrounds and extensive use of creamy tiling create a practical coordinated scheme, while smooth surfaces conceal generous storage space. Still, it looks far from clinical – filtered light through a simple drapery lends warmth to the color scheme and softens the hard lines of modern fixtures.

Soft and filtered
The white curtain, caught high and tied back, hangs from a white curtain rod. It filters the daylight that floods into the bright room.

Good lighting
Old-fashioned glass ceiling lights provide diffused general lighting, while a warm fluorescent strip lights up the vanity mirror with a golden light – perfectly functional yet not too strong for early morning.

Strip lighting used for shaving and making-up should be wide enough to cast light on the sides of the face as well as the front.

Cream and white
Pale colors help to create a sense of light and space. Matte cream tiles, fluffy creamy towels and simple white fixtures are complemented by touches of gleaming chrome.

A painted wood molding forms a neat defining line between wall tiles below and fresh white paint above.

Plant pots
The white flowering plants on the deep windowsill add a touch of green to the cream and white scheme.

The porcelain soup tureen is an attractive alternative to a traditional plant pot – and a good choice for a small space. Several plants can be neatly grouped together and take up little room.

Tiled surfaces
The floor, tub and much of the walls are covered in ceramic tiles for a clean coordinated look. Tiles offer excellent resistance to moisture and are easy to maintain, making them ideal for a bathroom.

Never use highly glazed tiles for flooring – they get very slippery when wet. Instead, use non-slip tiles especially designed for bathroom and kitchen use.

Space-saver
A freestanding towel rack provides lots of hanging space for towels and has the advantage of being movable. In addition, there's a rod underneath the vanity countertop on which wet towels can be dried.

Good storage
The lavatory alcove is surrounded by streamlined storage units, including a good-sized linen cupboard. Built in a continuous line, the units look neat and uncluttered.

THE COUNTRY LOOK

A small bathroom with a floral theme. The pale mushroom-colored walls are decorated with blossom motifs taken from the floral patterned fabric used for the ruched Austrian blind, while potted plants and cut flowers provide a fresh contrast.

Framed floral prints, wooden shelves and ornamental objects make the room comfortable and extremely cozy.

Flower sprays
Random sprays of blossom on the wall echo the floral print of the blind. These were hand-painted, but you can achieve a similar effect by stenciling a motif onto the wall.

A frilly blind
The pleated Austrian blind, in a charming floral print, is outlined with a frill and sets the scene for the whole room.
Note how the frill is edged with a plum-covered braid that provides style and definition.

Marble top
A plain white lavatory is set off effectively by an attractive marble surround.
Marble is a classic bathroom luxury – use good-looking imitations, such as Corian, or marble-effect laminates, instead.

Light detail
Brass wall lights with frilled shades suit the pretty floral look of the room.

Hot towels
A towel rack connected to the hot water system adds auxiliary heat to the bathroom and keeps towels dry and warm at the same time.

A new face
A new bath panel can give an old fixture a completely new look. Bath panels are available ready-made or you can make your own. This panel has been painted cream, and then dragged with a honey-colored glaze.

Warm wood
This old-fashioned wooden toilet seat suits the style of the room – it's also warm and more comfortable to sit on than plastic! Wooden toilet seats are available new in either dark or light woods.

Boxed in
In a small room, keep unattractive plumbing out of sight. Here, pipes and toilet tank are neatly hidden behind a panel painted to match the cupboards under the lavatory. The resulting ledge provides a useful shelf for bottles and ornaments, as well as hand towels.

IN A NOSTALGIC MOOD

The atmosphere of times past is re-created here but given a new slant with a light and airy scheme that suits modern tastes. A traditional cast-iron tub, brass reproduction faucets, an old bamboo folding table and chair are complemented by a pastel scheme.

Display board
A collection of postcards and memorabilia displayed on a bulletin board looks just as good in a bathroom as it does in a kitchen, where it is usually found. Coloring the board to match the tub and adding a matching ribbon trellis turns a utilitarian idea into an attractive and witty 'picture.'

Brass faucets
Choose antique-style faucets for a roll-top tub. It is still possible to get old faucets from architectural salvage companies. There are also numerous reproductions of period designs on the market.

Posters
Posters are an inexpensive way to decorate walls and the wide range of designs available makes it possible to find something to suit most situations. Here, they are linked to the scheme by their subject and because they have been mounted to match the display board. Ribbon corners give a feeling of a holiday album.

Border detail
Softly patterned walls are an excellent foil for posters and are made more interesting by adding a wallpaper border. Positioning this some way above the tub visually separates the 'business' area of the room from the wall decoration of bulletin board and posters.

Furniture and floor
An old lightweight bamboo table and chair, sisal matting and a cotton rug give an air of informality that suits the relaxed mood of this light and breezy room.

Stylized shell
The simple single-color stenciled design on the tub continues the seaside theme set by the travel posters. The fan motif on the border has been modified into a fan-shaped shell.

Old-style tub
You can give an old-fashioned roll-top tub up-to-date chic by painting the outside to fit in with your color scheme. Add a stenciled design for an individual touch.

Cushions
Cushions are a simple device for giving the finishing touch to a scheme by adding color, pattern or style accents. Here the stencil motif appears again in satin cushions shaped and quilted to represent shells.

A MARINE THEME

In this bathroom the feeling of sea and shore has been created around modern sand-colored fixtures.

The walls are lined with tongue-and-groove boards that have been painted a pretty soft blue-green to represent the sea. The carpet has been chosen to pick up the gold-beige of the room.

Stencils play a prominent part in this scheme, creating a border of foaming waves around ceiling and baseboard, decorating walls with shells and fishes.

Shells and fishes
Stencils in the shape of scallop shells, fishes and waves relieve the solid expanse of color on the walls.

Colors as well as motifs evoke the sea and shore. Shells and fishes are in a similar sandy shade to that of the bathroom furnishings and carpet; the waves are the dark blue-green of a rather stormy sea.

Wooden fascia
The deep wooden fascia, made of tongue-and-groove boards and painted to match the walls, lines up with the built-in cupboards and the edge of the bath. It gives the room a finished look and makes the bath seem much more private.

Round mirror
The white porthole-shaped mirror has a deep outline made of a delicate looking plastic which has a shell-like color.

Shower screen
A fixed screen is an efficient choice and more in keeping than a shower curtain which could look fussy in this room.

Wood paneling
Tongue-and-groove boards, fixed to a framework of battens, give the walls an interesting texture and have a nautical appeal.

The aquamarine color suggests the sea in summer with sunlight filtering through.

Fixtures and flooring
The bathroom fixtures and the carpet are in closely related gold-beige tones that bring to mind a warm sandy beach.

Lace curtain
The choice of a plain glass window, with its cream lace half-curtain and the view of foliage outside, prevents the room from becoming too austere.

A STREAMLINED BATHROOM

A windowless bathroom could be dark and rather oppressive. In this room the problem has been overcome by the careful choice of an almost all-white scheme so that fixtures blend in with the walls, floor and ceiling. Because white gives maximum light reflection, the bathroom looks light and everything seems much bigger and more spacious than it actually is.

Small amounts of strong red in contrast to the white and clever use of mirrors and glass all help to add more interest to the room scheme.

Hair dryer
This modern wall-mounted hair dryer is conveniently placed for use. It fits in with the slightly futuristic look of the whole room.

Mirror trickery
There are two narrow strips of mirror: on the wall and at the bottom of the bath panel. These help make the room look longer and lighter and reflect maximum light.

White background
Coloring the whole shell of the room in light-reflecting white and choosing white plumbing fixtures helps to make the room look light and spacious.

Glass shelves
Floor-to-ceiling open glass shelves house a supply of towels and toiletries. These shelves offer as much storage as a tall closet and blend well with the rest of the room.

Wall-mounted lavatory
This lavatory is wall-mounted and cantilevered, which means the plumbing is hidden behind paneling. This gives you maximum floor space.

Modular bathroom furniture
This neat wall unit has been bought as a complete package to include double lavatories, mirrored wall cabinet, and overhead light. It packs maximum activities into minimum space.

Stark contrast
Splashes of red add dramatic interest to an otherwise monochromatic color scheme. This only works well if the splashes of red are all the same shade like the laundry bag, bath mat, faucets and fittings.

CREATING A GARDEN MOOD

A ground floor room and a glass-roofed addition have been built to create a bathroom/dressing room with a look of luxury. The sloping glazed roof makes the room seem open and light and gives it a conservatory atmosphere. The room theme stems from this.

The color scheme is green and white and a trellis pattern is repeated throughout the room on the walls and curtains to reflect the garden theme. Old-fashioned fixtures and fittings are more suited to the relaxed mood of this room than modern ones.

Panels and border
Painting the wall panels and border green and covering them with white trellis gives a distinct impression of an arbor. To achieve this you could use garden trellis.

Climbing flowers
When these pretty flower-strewn patterned curtains are drawn the look of the garden is still retained in the bathroom.

Unfitted look
An old-fashioned rolltop tub, free-standing towel horse, brass faucets and brass fittings make the bathroom look and feel cozy and 'lived-in.'

Reflections
Two large mirrors, framed by trellis, add to the feeling of space and light and appear to give glimpses of a whole suite of other garden rooms.

Washstand look
Marble top and brass faucets give this vanity unit something of the look of a washstand, which works well with the old-style bath and accessories. With its roomy cupboard underneath it is also a practical choice. The lavatory is undermounted below the countertop surface so there is no lip under which soap and dirt can collect. It is important, however, to make sure the basin is fitted and sealed properly.

Floor tiles
Unpolished terra-cotta floor tiles work well with the room's conservatory theme. Their old-fashioned look complements the Victorian bath and towel horse.

Painted tub
Painting the outside of the tub in a light terra-cotta color with a matte, marble-effect finish is in perfect harmony with the earthy shades of the floor tiles.

BATHTUBS AND LAVATORIES

Buying bath fixtures is an important step
– they usually have to last a lifetime –
so consider your options carefully.

This chapter deals with tubs and lavatories while the following chapters look at toilets, bidets, showers and accessories.

First and foremost the tubs and lavatories in your house should reflect the washing habits and needs of your family. **Shape and size** are therefore important to get right; if members of your family are tall or you have children who bathe together, consider a larger-than-usual tub. If a lavatory is too shallow, when the faucets are turned on, the water will just splash straight out. If you plan to wash clothes in your lavatory, make sure that it is deep and large enough for

this. It should also be on a pedestal rather than wall hung, as this gives it extra strength to take the strain of pressing and washing in it.

Extras Check if the front and side panels are inclusive in the price of the tub. With the rectangular-shaped standard tubs they are usually extra. Decide if you need to buy the panels. You may want to continue the floor covering in your bathroom up the side of the tub or even panel the apron with decorative tiles.

Faucet selections are optional and can be quite expensive – especially the

more modern ones. Check where the faucet holes are in the tub or lavatory to make sure they suit the layout of your bathroom. Ask if you can choose where they are located. And if you are going to install a shower over the tub, check that the bath surface is non-slip.

Plumbing Consult a plumber early in your planning or you could end up buying an inexpensive and cheerful bathroom suite only to have to spend much more money solving plumbing problems. Make sure the plumber is well established and try to find one who is licensed.

MATERIALS USED

Enamel on cast iron or steel Cast iron is the traditional base material for tubs, but these days, steel is a cheaper and lighter alternative. The tub shape is molded from iron or steel and it is either sprayed with or dipped in porcelain enamel or vitreous china and fired in a furnace. This gives the tub a smooth, and hygienic surface and results in a rigid and very long lasting tub. It is, however, cold to the touch.

Use a non-abrasive bath cleaner to clean. Treat with care, as enamel can chip off and can only be repaired by re-enameling the whole tub.

Acrylic is easy to mold and so is ideal for making

interesting and unusual-shaped tubs. (There are very few acrylic lavatories available.) The acrylic itself is reinforced with fiberglass to give it strength and mounted onto a galvanized steel frame. It makes light, easy-to-install tubs, which are warm to the touch, but can be scratched. Check the thickness of the acrylic – if it is too thin, it tends to crack and split – the quality is reflected in the price.

Clean with a liquid cleaner. Never use harsh abrasives. Remove stains with spray cleaner or soap. Slight scratches can be smoothed out with liquid auto polish.

Fiberglass Tubs made of fiberglass make up a small but luxury end of the market. They are

built by hand in layers on a mold and, as only the top layer is coated with color, any deep scratch shows up, revealing the base color. They are warm, light and relatively easy to install. Only use liquid cleaners and avoid abrasives, which can remove the surface color.

Vitreous china is the primary material used to make lavatories. It is a clay that is fired in a kiln at a very high temperature and then glazed to give it a tough and hygienic seal. It is long lasting but care must be taken not to drop heavy objects in the bowl as the china is liable to crack or chip. With age the glaze will gradually begin to craze (develop fine cracks). Clean with mild detergent and avoid abrasives.

TUB SHAPES

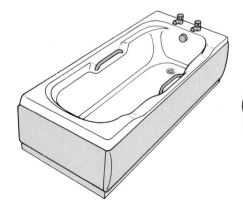

STANDARD RECTANGULAR

Style The standard size is 60in. × 30in., but there are larger and smaller versions on the market. If you are going to shower in the tub, the flatter the bottom, the better.
In use These are usually installed in a corner, but it is possible to install them at right angles to a wall, allowing access to the tub from both sides.

CORNER

Style These are usually made of acrylic because it molds into shapes so easily. Allow a 54in. × 54in. space for a corner tub in your bathroom.
In use Look for models with built-in shelf/seat ledges. Corner tubs hold slightly more water than the average tub.

CONTOURED

Style Usually made in acrylic, these tubs are shaped or waisted in the middle, tracing the outline of a human body.
In use They are very comfortable and are more economical with hot water than the standard shaped tub.

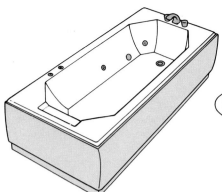
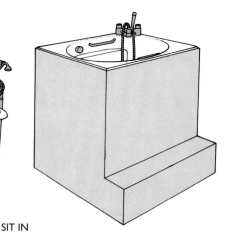

WHIRLPOOL
Style Also known as spas or Jacuzzis. Small nozzles set in sides of the tub pump out water under pressure into the tub when it is full. They are more expensive than ordinary units.
In use Very relaxing especially after hard physical exercise, as the movement of the water massages the body.

TRADITIONAL
Style This old Victorian-shaped, freestanding tub is enjoying a revival. It usually stands on small ball and claw legs. Although original cast iron models are still available, reproduction fiberglass types are cheaper.
In use Look for reproduction Victorian-style freestanding faucets to complement this tub.

SIT IN
Style This squat, square tub mimics the Oriental soaking tub. It is ideal for the small bathroom and easily doubles as a shower.
In use It has one or two built-in seats. Ideal for the elderly or disabled.

LAVATORY SHAPES

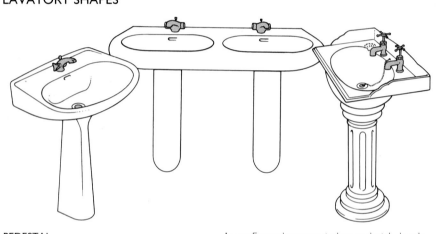

PEDESTAL
Style A pedestal lavatory is made up of two pieces – the bowl and pedestal. The pedestal is a supportive system, which in turn hides the plumbing. It is available in many shapes and sizes, old and new styles. There are even double pedestals, supporting twin bowls for a large or master bathroom.

In use Even when mounted on pedestals, bowls still need to be installed on the wall. One of their disadvantages is that, on average, they stand around 20-30in. high, so the height is fixed. This is too high for most young children. The pedestal does, however, take up floor space, which could in smaller bathrooms be put to much better use.

COLOR
Many of the colors for tubs and basins are standard colors, which means many different fixture manufacturers may produce identical or very similar colors. This also applies to tile manufacturers, so you should have little trouble in finding tiles to match your selection.

The same color on a china lavatory can vary when reproduced on an acrylic tub. Remember that the color of your fixtures will dictate your bathroom color scheme – white is the most versatile as it tends to blend well with most other colors. Dark colors will show stains, soap marks and hard water deposits.

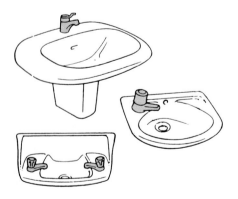

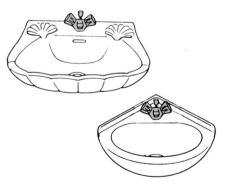

WALL MOUNTED
Style These lavatories vary from larger-than-standard size to tiny hand rinse units designed only for powder rooms. They are hung from the wall so the pipes are usually exposed, although you can buy a wall-hung pedestal.
In use They are especially good where floor space is limited.

COUNTERTOP LAVATORIES
Style These come in a variety of shapes to be installed into countertops or vanity units. They are also available integrally molded as a unit in ceramic, acrylic or Corian.
In use Cupboards or vanity units into which these lavatories are set hide plumbing and provide extra bathroom storage space.

UNUSUAL SHAPES
Style Lavatories come in many different shapes and sizes. A triangular-shaped unit fits neatly into the corner of your bathroom so is practical and space saving. Other shapes can simply be installed for decorative purposes.
In use For unusual-shaped lavatories, especially corner-shaped units, there is often no room for faucets, so consider installing them on wall above.

FAUCETS, TOILETS AND BIDETS

The style and shape of plumbing fixtures and the types of faucets that you choose, set the whole mood of your bathroom.

Although the modern bathroom is often one of the smaller rooms in a house, it is one of the most frequently used. Space should be handled carefully as there are a definite number of essential bathroom fixtures; the toilet is one of them. The bidet, so popular in Europe, is becoming more common in the U.S. and is usually included in bathroom sets.

The variety of bathroom faucets on the market is growing and becoming ever more sophisticated.

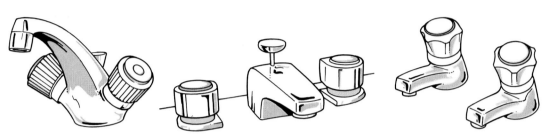

FAUCETS

If you are replacing faucets, your choice is restricted by the size and number of tapholes provided in your tub, lavatory or bidet. But if you are starting from scratch, you can choose from faucets of all different shapes and styles.

There are a variety of finishes available; from the conventional chrome-plated to stainless steel, brass and gold, as well as colored plastic taps.

Make sure your faucet selections meet local code requirements. This will guarantee that the faucet allows water to pass through at an acceptable flow rate. All faucets should satisfy your local water authority's requirements, which safeguard against water wastage or contamination. For more information, contact your local building department.

MIXING FAUCETS

Style This mixes the hot and cold water supply into one central spout. There are basically two mixer types: the dual flow mixer faucet appears to mix both hot and cold water through a central spout, but in fact each supply runs along its own separate channel in the tap/spout. A 'true' mixer really does mix hot and cold together, but it must be installed by a plumber so

both are of equal pressure.

In use A mixer faucet, which has to be plumbed into the tub, lavatory or bidet, through just one taphole, is known as a monobloc mixer, (above left). A three-piece mixer, (above), can only be fitted to fixtures with three tapholes; one for the spout and two holes for the valves. Both the dual flow and 'true' mixer come as either monoblocs, three-piece or "centerset" designs.

PILLAR TAPS

Style This is the old-fashioned type of tap, usually bought in a pair – one for the cold water, the other for the hot. The water supply pipe to the pillar tap usually comes from below, so the tap must be mounted on a horizontal surface such as a tub or lavatory rim.

In use The modern pillar taps are usually much smaller and neater than the traditional ones.

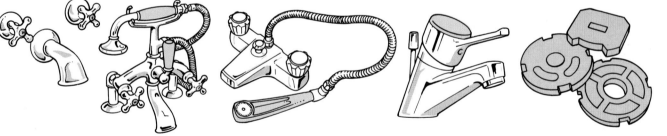

TUB VALVES

Style Tub valves also come as monoblocs and two- or three-piece types. Many come with shower hose and diverter lever to channel water from the spout through the hose and out the shower head.

In use With a three-piece mixer, the two valves can be set on the rim of the tub and the spout may be set lower down on the inside panel of the tub. Look for reproduction Victorian valves for freestanding tubs.

SINGLE-LEVER FAUCET

Style On this type of faucet a lever controls the flow of water. Usually the more the lever is raised, the greater the flow of water. Most types are in fact mixer valves, so the lever moves to the left or right

to give hot or cold water.

In use Most washer faucets are being replaced by ceramic disc faucets (shown enlarged above). Durable and more resistant to lime scale, they form a watertight seal in the valve to avoid a problem with dripping.

BIDET VALVE

Style The most basic faucet for the bidet just mixes hot and cold water. Look for units with spouts that swivel to allow more room for washing. Some bidet faucets offer

adjustable nozzles, to give a directional spray (douche).

In use If installing a bidet mixer, check with your water authority or plumber that it conforms to code regulations.

DRAINS

Lavatory and tub water is let out through a drain (or plug hole). The traditional drain is plugged with a plastic or rubber plug hanging on a chain from the overflow outlet.

The more modern pop-up drain does away with a plug on a chain. When a lever (usually part of the tap) is pressed or alternatively when a knob (set in the bath panel) is turned, a lid or cover over the waste automatically pops up to let out the water.

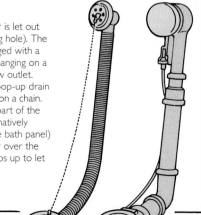

TOILETS

A toilet is usually made of vitreous china, because it is non-porous and therefore hygienic. Toilets consist of a bowl containing water and a tank that holds the water for flushing away waste.

The flush is operated by a handle or similar device.

Wash-down This is the most common flushing mechanism. It uses a large flow of water that scours the whole inner surface of the bowl and is powerful enough to discharge the contents of the bowl. It is efficient but can be rather noisy.

Syphon flush This is an alternative flushing method. It operates by syphoning (drawing out) the water. It is quiet and more efficient.

Pumping unit (macerator) This is a device that can be fitted to a toilet to shred and pump the discharge electronically. It flushes waste through a much narrower pipe (small diameter), so the toilet can be installed almost anywhere in the house because the narrower pipe is easily run behind walls. Macerators are less commonly used.

Traps Like all other bathroom fixtures, the toilet bowl has a trap (a bend in the outpipe), which holds water to form a seal, preventing sewer gases from coming into the house. As the trap is an integral part of the waste pipe on your toilet, check which type you need.

If the waste pipe disappears straight into the wall behind the toilet, a horizontal or P-trap is required, if it disappears into the floor below, buy an S-trap unit.

Tanks, waste pipes and plumbing can be hidden behind a false wall.

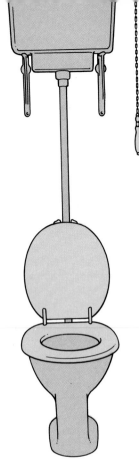

CLOSE COUPLED
Style A close-coupled toilet incorporates tank and bowl in a single construction.
In use This saves space and gives a very neat appearance.

BACK TO THE WALL
Style The outlet connenctions (waste pipe, for example) are completely contained in the ceramic shape of the toilet.
In use The overall appearance is neat and its compact shape is easy to clean around.

WALL HUNG
Style This toilet is mounted on an invisible bracket that runs below the floor and behind the wall.
In use This leaves the floor area around the toilet completely clear. It may be complemented by a ducted boxed-in tank.

OVERHEAD
Style This is the traditional arrangement – the tank is set high on the wall above the bowl. They are joined by a length of waste pipe.
In use This has been almost totally updated by the low-level tank – the tank is mounted just above the bowl joined by a shorter pipe called the flushbend.

BIDETS

The bidet is a low-level wash basin for personal hygiene. It is also just the right height for children to wash in and, it is sometimes used as a foot bath.

Most bidets are made from vitreous china to complement the shapes and colors of the lavatory and bidet.

Over-the-rim A bidet is supplied by both hot and cold running water and the basic type is filled over-the-rim in the same way as a lavatory is filled.

Below-the-rim The more sophisticated and expensive models are filled by a method called below-the-rim, which means that the bidet is warmer to sit on than the over-the-rim type, as a stream of hot water is sent around the rim before the bowl is filled, some also have a douche option.

Before buying, check with your plumbing inspector that it conforms to code, as below-the-rim models are prohibited by some authorities.

WALL HUNG
Style All the plumbing for the bidet is ducted (concealed behind a panel or false wall).
In use A wall-hung bidet is usually chosen to match a wall-hung toilet.

FREESTANDING
Style The plumbing is visible, like a low level toilet.
In use This should be set at the same height as the toilet.

SIZES AND POSITIONING
Space shortage is a common problem in a bathroom and the positioning of toilets and bidets is often restricted because of plumbing requirements.

Toilets The size of a toilet varies from one manufacturer to another. But as a guideline the bowl should be at a height to be comfortable to sit on. Allow for a floor space of about 54in. × 27in. wide for a toilet with a tank. This gives you enough space not to feel cramped using it. The bowl must be covered with a wooden or plastic seat.

On the modern low-level toilet, the tank is usually about 24-36in. high. The high-level tank is more like 72in. high.

A low-level toilet takes up more room than a high-level, because the tank sits closely above the bowl so the bowl is further forward than if the tank is 72in. above it.

Less space can be used up with a low-level toilet if you buy a one-piece unit.

Bidets A bidet is usually the same height as the toilet – about 15in. It should be located as near to the toilet as possible.

WATER SUPPLIES
Regulations for the plumbing installations of bidets vary from locality to locality. Your plumber should advise you on local requirements, but generally the over-the-rim type is quite straight forward to install, while the below-the-rim type needs special installation to stop what is known as back syphonage, which can cause water contamination.

This type of bidet must have its own cold water supply pipe running directly from the cold water source and no other pipes or fittings should be connected.

The hot water supply must run from the highest pipe taken off the hot water heater and again no other pipes or fittings should be connected to it. All plumbing systems require that waste water is discharged via the soil pipe.

CHOOSING A SHOWER

Showering has many advantages — perhaps the most important is that it's a quick, easy and economical way to wash.

A shower uses one-fifth of the water used to run a bath, which not only saves on water, but also on heating bills. It is also quicker to shower than to bathe and, if you choose to install a shower instead of a tub, it takes up much less floor space. Many people believe that showering is more hygienic than soaking in a tub, as soap and grime are constantly being rinsed away in the shower by clean, running water. Follow our guidelines on how to choose the best shower for your home.

TYPES OF SHOWERS

When it comes to shower stall units, there are three basic types: the prefabricated, one-piece type; the custom-built stall with a prefabricated shower pan; or the custom-built stall with a custom-built shower pan. Shower stalls are available without a threshold for wheelchair use.

The **prefabricated** type is the easiest to install and is available in a variety of colors, sizes and shapes. However, most are square or rectangular consisting of an open side for a doorway. Neo-angle units, those that fit into the corners of bathrooms, have a diagonal front. The walls of all prefabricated units must be attached to sturdy framing as they are not structural.

Fiberglass is the most commonly used material for shower stalls. The surface is finished with acrylic or another kind of plastic, which should be cleaned with a non-abrasive cleanser. No tiling is required.

If your bathroom requires, look for units that have ceilings. Luxury

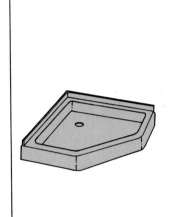
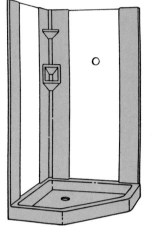

units come with an optional top so that they can be used as steam rooms. Most models require that you buy the doors to the shower separately.

Prefabricated pans can be used with either prefabricated or custom-made shower stall units. They are available in moldings

made of plastic, terrazzo or chipped stone, the latter being the most substantial looking and feeling. Color options are available; most come with skid-resistant floors.

Custom-made shower stalls offer creative flexibility. The only constraints placed on custom-made shower stalls are the bathroom

dimensions and the material in which the stall is made. Carefully plan the dimensions of the new shower, considering a more open space with a high ceiling or a smaller, cozier enclosure. Any material that is waterproof and easily maintained, such as marble or glass block, can be used for the walls.

POSITIONING YOUR SHOWER

Over the tub Any type of shower can be installed over a tub. It is the obvious location as the drainage for the shower water is already there. As you have to stand in the tub, the base should be as flat and wide as possible and preferably have a non-skid finish. Otherwise, buy a non-skid shower mat to stand on.

Showering in the tub usually gives you more space to stand away from the shower spray, so it is possible to shower without, for example, getting your hair wet.

Corner or alcove shower stall If you don't want a shower over the tub, then a stall shower is another choice. This means you can have your shower in another room.

With a corner stall, the two adjacent walls, which form the inside of the shower, need to be totally waterproof. Tiled walls are ideal, as long as the grout used in between the tiles is waterproof. With alcove showers, all three of the walls need to be waterproof.

Freestanding units These can be made of plastic, strengthened safety glass or coated steel. They come with four panels, shower pan, plumbing and fittings, so you don't

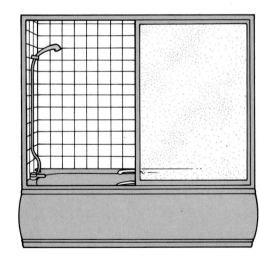
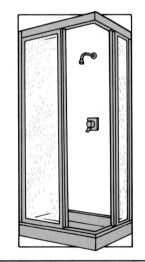

have to rely on any of the interior walls as frames. Some have tops, too, to prevent vapor from escaping and causing condensation in the room. Kit forms are often the cheapest way to buy them.

As long as there is enough clearance for the door, a shower stall can be positioned almost anywhere in the bathroom. When choosing a location keep these conditions in mind: natural light, ventilation, access to towels and space to towel off.

SHOWER PANS

A shower pan is the base that you stand in if you have a corner/alcove or separate shower stall unit.

It can be made from vitreous china, fiberglass, acrylic or vitreous enameled steel, in colors to match bathroom fixtures.

On average, a tray measures between 30in. and 36in. square,

although bigger or smaller sizes in different shapes, including neo-angle ones for corner showers, are available.

If you plan to tile the walls around the shower pan, look for one with a special tiling lip. If the shower is to replace a tub, consider a shower pan with a foot well and molded-in seat so you can shower sitting down.

ENCLOSURES

Shower curtains These are an easy-to-fit and relatively inexpensive shower enclosure. They are waterproof, washable or can be wiped down and are usually made from PVC, nylon, or coated cotton. Many are treated so they won't become moldy.

However, you can hang a shower curtain made of any fabric if you line the side that receives most of the splashing with a plastic curtain. Look for non-rusting hooks and eyelets.

Curtains hang from rods or poles made of a light, rust-proof material such as aluminum or plastic. They can be fastened to the wall with screws and brackets or come spring-loaded so the pole lodges itself firmly in-between two walls. Curtains can form either one, two, or three sides of an over-the-tub or corner/alcove shower stall.

Bath screens are used with over-the-tub showers as alternatives to curtains. They are usually made of glass or plastic. The screen is attached to the side of the tub to keep the shower water from splashing over the edge. Some screens run along half the length of the tub. They can be fixed or hinged, so they can be swiveled to allow the user easier entry. Others are made in two or three separate pieces, each hinged together to fold like a pleat.

Another variety is the sliding enclosure; two doors run along the entire length of the tub and slide backwards and forwards in a track. **Shower screens and doors** Screens for shower stall cubicles are usually made from safety glass or plastic. Shower doors may hinge, pivot, slide or fold open and shut.

SHOWER HEADS

The shower head, (also known as a head shower if it can be detached from the wall and hand held), should be mounted above the height of the user, or alternatively at shoulder level.
Magnetic head A magnetic shower head supplied with water via a flexible hose, can be positioned anywhere on the walls of a steel shower unit.
Clip-on head This shower head with a flexible hose is fastened by a clip so it can be detached.
Head on slide rail Many showers have the shower head on a slide rail. The angle of the spray can be adjusted, as well as the height, by sliding the handshower up and down the rail. The head is on a flexible hose so it can be hand held.
Brush head There are shower heads on the market that are like a brush. They can be detached and used while still spraying water.
Fixed head This means the height of the shower is permanently fixed, although the head can be swiveled to alter the angle of the spray. It is plumbed to a specific height and the pipework to the head is usually ducted (run behind panels or tiling). There are many different styles.
Body spray and jets Some luxury freestanding shower units not only spray water at the user via a shower head, but also via a series of pipes or individual spray heads mounted at various locations.

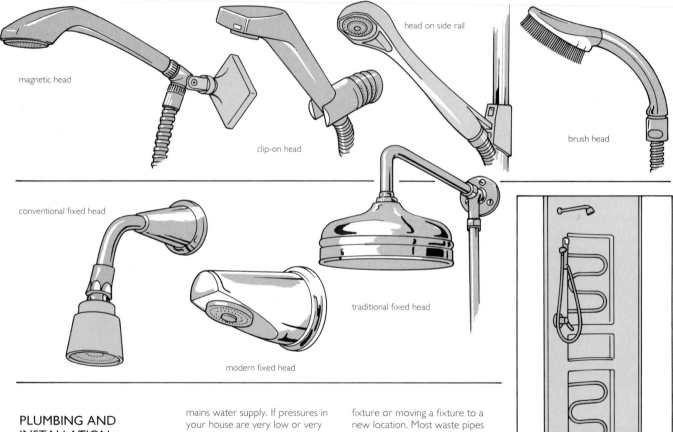

magnetic head

clip-on head

head on side rail

brush head

conventional fixed head

modern fixed head

traditional fixed head

body spray

PLUMBING AND INSTALLATION

Many showers only operate if there is sufficient water pressure. Your plumber should be able to advise you on this, and your local water authority should be able to tell you the pressure of your incoming mains water supply. If pressures in your house are very low or very high, check what pressures the shower valve requires before making a purchase.

Before installing a new shower, the drainpipes and vent pipes must be considered. Consult a plumber when considering a new plumbing fixture or moving a fixture to a new location. Most waste pipes from separate shower pans should be reasonably close to the soil pipe.

SHOWER SAFETY

Water and soap make a slippery combination, so a grab rail in the wall of the shower area is useful – especially for the elderly or infirm.

Sliding shower doors or those hinged to open inwards prevent drips on the floor in front of the shower – and may cut down the risk of slipping. Check your local building authority to see if inward opening shower doors are allowed.

A soap dish recessed into the wall is also a sensible feature. Look for a soap dish that clips on to the showerhead slide rail (right), so it can be raised or lowered to suit the user.

A shower seat is especially useful for the elderly or disabled to sit on while taking a shower. It does not have to be built into the shower wall, but can be bought as a ready-made fitting (far right). The plastic slatted seat folds up flush against the wall when not in use.

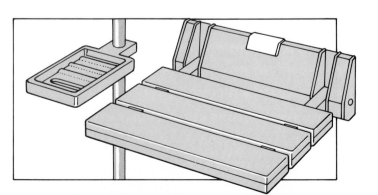

BATHROOM ACCESSORIES

A bathroom wouldn't function properly without the simple accessories that make bath times so much easier.

As well as being attractive, bathroom accessories should be practical additions to your bathroom, for keeping a whole host of items tidy and easily accessible.

Most items can be chosen from large varieties and are usually made from easy-to-clean materials – choose from plastic, glass, china, wood, brass, stainless steel and chrome. Some accessories even come with gold plating. There are prices to suit everyone, from a few dollars to thousands of dollars.

The biggest choice of accessories comes in the wall-mounted styles. You'll find toilet tissue holders, toothbrush holders, towel and robe hooks, towel bars and rings, shelves, soap dishes and wall cabinets. In addition, there are free-standing accessories such as toilet brushes, garbage bins and towel racks.

STORAGE ACCESSORIES
Toiletries, spare toilet tissue, medicine and cleaning equipment can either be displayed on wall-mounted shelving or stored away inside a cupboard. A good-size bathroom cabinet with a mirror on the front is invaluable – especially if it has an integral light and an electrical outlet nearby.

Cheaper models are molded plastic towel bars made especially to hang on the wall above the tub or lavatory. Most have shelves, but some also incorporate useful additions such as toothbrush holders and cup holders.

TOILET ACCESSORIES
Give your toilet a new look by changing the old seat for a new one, or cover it with a fabric cover. Most covers come as a set with a shaped toilet mat, and optional bath mat.

MATERIALS
Plastic accessories come in a variety of pastel, primary and neutral shades to coordinate with the most popular plumbingware colors.

Wood accessories come in many shades, but tend toward pine to match light, country-style rooms, and dark oak, which is often used with china and brass for a traditional feel.

Metal Least expensive of all is chrome but you can choose from bronze, pewter, brass and stainless steel (as well as gold plate).

Ceramic If made by a plumbingware manufacturer, ceramic accessories should match your fixtures exactly. If you are planning to tile your walls, there are some pretty ceramic accessories made to fit into a standard tile space; others are simply surface-mounted.

TYPES OF ACCESSORIES

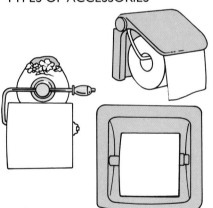

TOILET TISSUE HOLDER
Style A metal, plastic or wooden dowel that slips through the center of the toilet roll. Some are recessed into the wall and others come with covers as well.
In use Check that the holder allows the toilet tissue to run freely – some designs need two hands to use them and are less convenient.

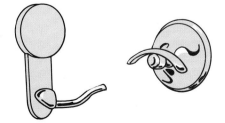

ROBE HOOK
Style Small hook, usually made of wood, metal or plastic, attached to the wall on a bracket.
In use For hanging dressing gowns or robes while in the bathroom.

TOWEL BAR
Style Can be wall mounted, freestanding or attached to plumbing. They come in plastic, wood or a range of different metals. Heated versions are also available.
In use It's a good idea to place the bar above a radiator so that wet towels can dry while they are hanging – less costly than a heated rack.

TOWEL RACK
Style A small bank of hooks or knobs.
In use Position the rack over the tub to catch drips from wet towels – over the radiator is a viable alternative.

TOWEL RING
Style A round or semi-circular ring made of wood, metal or plastic which is wall mounted or attached to a vanity unit.
In use Ideal to use where space is limited. Place close to the lavatory or on a door.
Watchpoint Towels that are not hung flat tend to dry more slowly.

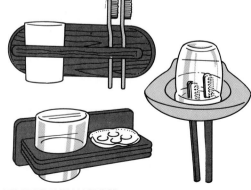

TOOTHBRUSH HOLDER
Style A small slotted rack to hold toothbrushes. Many holders incorporate a space for a glass or mug and a tube of toothpaste.
In use A handy way of keeping toothbrushes clean and ready to use.

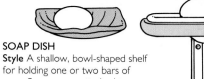
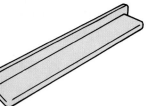

SOAP DISH

Style A shallow, bowl-shaped shelf for holding one or two bars of soap. Some come attached to a wall tile and others can be recessed into a wall.

In use Position within easy reach beside the tub or lavatory where wet soap will not fall onto the floor.

Watchpoint Look for a mesh design or one with a ridged base that will stop the soap from becoming soft.

SHELVES

Style Glass, plastic, metal or wooden storage shelves with an ornate or discreetly hidden mounting bracket.

In use Position shelves below a mirror but above the lavatory, at the back of the tub or in a corner to hold bottles and jars.

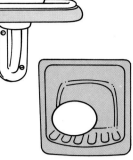

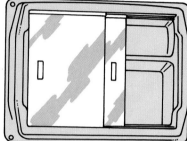

CABINETS

Style Molded from plastic or wood framed, most cabinets have one or more interior shelves. Some have mirrored doors, built-in lights and an electrical outlet. Corner models are available.

In use Position the cabinet where it won't be in the way – in a corner or above the lavatory are practical.

Watchpoint When storing medicine or cleaning products, choose a cabinet with a childproof lock.

SHOWER CADDIES

Style Made in a wire mesh or from plastic with drainage holes, these cabinets are designed for use in a shower since water can drain straight through them.

In use For holding soap, shampoo and washcloths while using the shower. Position so that you can easily reach it when showering: next to the shower unit is preferable to below it so that water doesn't soften the soap.

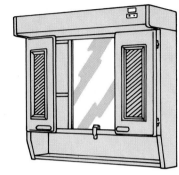

BATH SHELVES/CABINETS

Style Molded in one piece from plastic, these rigid storage holders are made in colors to match plumbingware and to fit alongside standard-size tubs.

In use Tall units can be fitted at the end of a tub or over a lavatory with space to hold toothbrushes and soap, as well as a shelf and a mirror. Long, thin versions are made to fit along the length of your tub to hold toiletries.

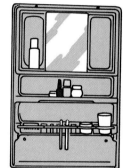

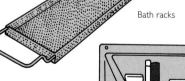

Bath racks

Bath bar

BATH RACK

Style Usually made of metal, often plastic-coated, the rack sits across the width of the tub and is used to hold bath sponges and toiletries.

In use Make sure your rack has holes punched in the base to allow water to drain away freely and keep the soap from becoming soggy.

BATH BAR

Style Long plastic unit designed to hang on the wall alongside the tub. For holding accessories such as toiletries, nail brushes and sponges. Many designs also incorporate a small mirror.

In use Locate on the wall next to the tub. Directly above is the most suitable place.

Watchpoint Not intended for freestanding tubs.

TOILET BRUSHES

Style A pot or stand with a detachable brush that is used for cleaning the toilet.

In use Some pots can be filled with disinfectant so that the brush can be sterilized when it is not in use. Since toilet brushes are usually placed next to the toilet, it is a good idea to choose a coordinating style and color.

TOILET SEAT

Style Many different styles of toilet seats are available in plastic, ceramic or wood. There is a huge range of colors and finishes to select from.

In use Each seat comes complete with mounting hardware so it's an easy job to remove the old one and install the new.

Watchpoint Not all seats fit all toilets, so measure carefully when choosing a replacement.

SLIP MAT

Style A square, oblong or oval rubber mat with suction pads on the bottom to hold it firmly in place on the tub or shower pan surface.

In use Lay a mat in a bath or shower tray to produce a safe and completely non-skid surface – especially useful for the very young or the elderly.

Watchpoint In a shower, make sure the mat doesn't cover the drain hole of the shower pan.

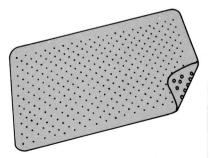

INDEX

PHOTOGRAPHIC CREDITS
American Olean Tile Co., 12 (top), 27, 29, 38 (bottom), 40 (bottom)
American Standard, 40-1, 44 (top)
Aqua Dial, 55 (bottom right)
Arcaid/Lucinda Lambton, 32 (bottom)
B&Q DIY Centres, 84
Berglen Tapmate, 46
BJ Alia, 64 (top)
Boots and Bathrooms, 4-5
Bosch, 43
Camera Press, 81
Caprez, 11 (bottom)
Century Shower Door, Inc. 72-3
Cover Plus from Woolworth, 20 (top), 34, 42 (bottom)
CP Hart, 28 (bottom)
Phillip H. Ennis Photography, 25, 30, 36, 39, 40-1, 60
EWA 24-5, 51 (bottom), 85
EWA/Michael Dunne, 75 (bottom), 86
EWA/Andreas von Einsiedel, 31
EWA/Clive Helm, 21 (bottom)
EWA/Rodney Hyett, 2-3, 74 (bottom), 80 (top)
EWA/Neil Lorimer, 28 (top)
EWA/Michael Nicholson, 35
EWA/Julian Nieman, 21 (top)
EWA/Spike Powell, 74 (top)
Fanfare 2000 by Fordham, 12 (bottom)
Fordham, 51 (top)
Grub Street, 38 (bottom)

H&R Johnson, 33
Harrod of Lowestoft, 58 (bottom)
Ideal Standard, 16, 18 (top)
Jalag, 26, 57 (top right), 73 (bottom)
Jalag/Peter Adams, 77
Kohler, 10 (top), 11 (top), 13 (top), 20 (bottom left), 32 (top), 52 (top right), 53, 69, 80 (left)
Mantaleda, 19
Marbodal of Sweden, 10 (bottom)
Melabee M. Miller, cover photograph, 6, 37 (bottom), 45 (bottom), 76, 79, 80
National Kitchen & Bath Association, 9, 38 (top), 72 (bottom)
National Magazine Co/Dennis Stone, 13 (bottom), 52 (top left)
National Magazine Co/William Douglas, 15
National magazine Co/Lucinda Lambton, 82
Next Interior, 60 (bottom)
Richard Paul, 61 (top)
Pinelog Products, 55 (top)
Pipe Dreams, 41, 54 (bottom)
Poggenpohl, 14
PWA International, 37 (top), 83
Rutt, 45 (top)
John Suett/Eaglemoss, 57 (bottom)
Smallbone, 50
Sommer Allibert, 48 (top)
Star Interiors, 42 (top)
Stelrad, 54 (top)
Superior Fireplace, 47, 58
Syndication International, 18 (bottom), 22, 24

(bottom), 52 (top right), 65, 70
Tilemart, 59
Jerry Tubby/Eaglemoss, 20 (bottom right)
Twyfords, 56 (bottom), 56-7, 78
Vymura, 52 (bottom)
Wickes Building Supplies Ltd, 48-49 (top)
Zess, 55 (bottom left)

DESIGNER CREDITS:
Baker Furniture, 10
Diane Boyer, ASID, 40-41 (top)
Ronald Budney, ASID, 32 (top)
Marlee Cashman, muralist, 25
Rosemarie Cicio, Rosemarie Cicio Interiors, 6
Country Floors, 36
Kathleen Dickleman, Cover photograph
Kathleen Donohue, CKD, 72 (bottom)
Rene Hennessey, 45 (bottom)
Perry Iannaconi, Studio for the Interior Arts, 37 (bottom)
KJS Interiors, 30 (top)
Joan Kay, 80
Victoria Leist, 38 (top)
Gail Pearlman, Loft Interiors, 76
Robert Perron, 44 (bottom)
Betty Jo Purvis, ASID, 13 (top)
Anna Salibello/Terra Designs, Inc., 60
Martha Sasso, 9
Richard Schlesinger Interior Design, 39
Karen Shapiro, 79